THE JOURNAL OF JULES RENARD

The Journal of

Jules Renard

EDITED AND TRANSLATED BY

LOUISE BOGAN AND ELIZABETH ROGET

Tin House Books

Originally published in France under the title *Journal* by Jules Renard

This translation was first published in the United States by George Braziller, Inc., 1964.

Tin House Books edition copyright © 2008

Published by Tin House Books, Portland, Oregon, and New York, New York
www.tinhouse.com

Distributed to the trade by Publishers Group West, 1700 Fourth St., Berkeley, CA 94710, www.pgw.com

Library of Congress Cataloging-in-Publication Data

Renard, Jules, 1864-1910.
    [Journal. English]
    The Journal of Jules Renard / edited and translated by Louise Bogan and Elizabeth Roget.
        p. cm.
    Includes bibliographical references and index.
    ISBN 978-0-9794198-7-4 (alk. paper)
    1. Renard, Jules, 1864-1910--Diaries. 2. Authors, French--19th century--Diaries. 3. Authors, French--20th century--Diaries. I. Bogan, Louise, 1897-1970. II. Roget, Elizabeth. III. Title.
    PQ2635.E48Z4613 2008
    840.1--dc22   2008019921

ISBN 10: 0-9794198-7-5

Interior design by Laura Shaw Design, Inc.

Printed in Canada

CONTENTS

It astounds us to come upon other egoists, as though we alone had the right to be selfish, and be filled with the eagerness to live.

In order to do certain crazy things, it is necessary to behave like a coachman who has let go of the reins and fallen asleep.

I can't get around this dilemma: I have a horror of troubles, but they whip me up, they make me talented. Peace and well-being, on the contrary, paralyze me. Either be a nobody, or everlastingly plagued.

I'm intelligent, more intelligent than many others. This is obvious, since I can read The Temptation of Saint Anthony *without falling asleep. But this intelligence is like water running, unknown, unused, in some region where no one has as yet built a mill. Yes, that is it: I have not yet found my mill. Shall I ever find it?*

[André Gide] is clean-shaven, has a cold in the nose and throat, an exaggerated jaw, eyes between two welts. He is in love with Oscar Wilde, whose photograph I perceive on the mantel: a fleshy gentleman, very refined, also clean-shaven, who has recently been discovered.

1892   49

At the café, [Verlaine] is addressed as "Maître" and "cher Maître," but he is worried, and wants to know what they did with his hat. He looks like a drunken god. All that is left of him is our cult. Above clothes in ruins—a yellow tie, an overcoat that must stick to his flesh in several places—a head out of building stone in process of demolition.

1893   58

Whenever I have talked to anyone at too great length, I am like a man who has drunk too much, and, ashamed, doesn't know where to put himself.

1894   66

[Lautrec] often mentions small men, while seeming to say: "And I'm not as small as all that!" He has a room in a "house," is on good terms with all the ladies, who have feelings of a fineness unknown to honest women, and who pose admirably. He also owns a convent, and he goes from the convent to the "house."

1895   77

I desire nothing from the past. I do not count on the future. The present is enough for me. I am a happy man, for I have renounced happiness.

1896   89

Sarah Bernhardt. When she comes down the winding staircase of the hotel, it looks as though she was standing still, while the staircase turns around her.

1897   104

"I have a hundred clippings," I say, "testifying to the success of Plaisir de Rompre." Why do I say a hundred, when I know quite well there are not over seventy?

1898   123

I turn home, my heart filled with anguish because I have watched the sun set and heard the birds sing, and because I shall have had so few days on this earth I love, and there are so many dead before me.

1899   133

I am not content with intermittent life: I must have life at each instant.

1900 142

I, I, not an enthusiast? A few notes of music, the sound of flowing water, the wind in the leaves, and my poor heart runs over with tears, with real tears—yes, yes!

1901 155

We no longer know what love is. The thing itself is lost, drowned in a verbal deluge. It is impossible to come through to reality, which should be simple and clear.

1902 167

As long as thinkers cannot tell me what life and death are, I shall not give a good goddamn for their thoughts.

1903 176

You say I am an atheist, because we do not search for God in the same manner; or rather, you believe you have found Him. I congratulate you. I am still searching for Him. I shall search for Him ten, twenty years, if He lends me life.

1904 192

How quickly one could lose one's head! Any moment, there is nothing between us and death but the paper hoop of the clown. It should not be too difficult to jump through! We would not reappear, that is all.

1905 212

In order to work, you clear away the obligations in your life. No visits, no meals on the outside, no fencing or promenades. You will be able to work, to do fine things—and, on that wide gray sheet that is a day, your mind projects nothing.

1906 229

If I were to begin life again, I should want it as it was. I would only open my eyes a little more. I did not see properly, and I did not see everything in that little universe in which I was feeling my way.

1907 253

. . . one does not grow old. Where the heart is concerned, the fact is accepted, at least in matters of love. Well, it is the same with the mind. It always remains young. You do not understand life any more at forty than you did at twenty, but you are aware of this fact, and you admit it. To admit it is to remain young.

PREFACE

"Je lis avec ravissement le *Journal* de Jules Renard . . .
Il y a là, par moments, de l'excellent, du parfait; et parfois même,
ô surprise, de l'attendri . . ."

−André Gide, *Journal* (March 1927)

It is difficult to discover, given Jules Renard's steadily augmented reputation in France and elsewhere since his death in 1910, the reasons for the almost total neglect of his work in England and America. His chief fame in English-speaking countries came to be attached to the motion picture, released in the early thirties, based on *Poil de Carotte*, the extraordinary autobiographical *récit* first published in 1894 and later made into a one-act play by Renard in 1900. In France, his early novel, *L'Ecornifleur* (1892), is considered one of the great novels of the nineteenth century. His *Journal*, published in definitive form in 1935, was reissued in 1960 in the format of the *Bibliothèque de la Pléiade*−a series remarkable for its finely-produced editions of French classical literature. Critical praise of a high order has been tendered the author over the years. Albert Thibaudet in 1927 named Renard's *Journal inédit*, along with Gide's *Si le grain ne meurt*, as incontestably the two autobiographical masterpieces of the twentieth century.

Renard never in any manner attached himself to that *avant-garde* which was in process of formation in Paris in all the arts during his lifetime, and this separation from movements which were about to gather to themselves the most striking talents of the new century may well have kept his reputation apart from the mainstream of influence. Renard wrote plays for the theatres of the boulevards. He became a member of the *Académie Goncourt*, but was never closely in touch with the experimental or the extreme. Although he knew and liked Toulouse-Lautrec (who was to illustrate his *Histoires naturelles*), he took no interest when Maurice Ravel set parts of this most charming bestiary to music, not even to the extent of attending a first concert presentation.

It is one of Renard's central virtues that his mind and emotions continued to be refreshed by the air of his countryside—especially during the years—when he, like his father before him, became mayor of Chitry.

The keeping of a journal may become a futile and time-wasting occupation for a writer. Temptations toward the inconsequential detail, the vaporous idea and the self-regarding emotion are always present and can become overwhelming. Renard's *Journal*, from its beginning, shows a young writer who is consciously moving away from early mistakes, whose goal is cleanness of style and precision of language. We do not see him as an innovator, but as one who made restitution of certain classically severe effects which the French Romantics in their exuberance, and the Symbolists in their search for the extremes of musicality, had overlooked or ignored. It is possible, in the pages of the *Journal*, to watch Renard training himself, "independent of schools . . . how to reproduce in compressed and resistant [prose] life completely pure and completely simple"—his life and the life of others.

The atmosphere of the period was hardly propitious for this sort of truth-telling, or this sort of style. The great days of Symbolism were over—Mallarmé had died in 1898—and the central figures of the modem revolt in all the arts were still too young to have made their mark. A tired exoticism afflicted academic and "official" art, and poetry (no matter how feeble)—not prose—gave entrance to the *salons*. Renard's early apprenticeship writing reflects this atmosphere. But by 1890, when he was twenty-six, he had begun to put his youthful affectations and artificialities behind him for good; the *Journal*, from its first pages, abounds in mockery of the false, the half-observed, and the grandiose.

Renard's passion for factual truth and stylistic exactitude, once formed, remained central to his work throughout his career. This preoccupation never hardened into obsession; one of the great pleasures of reading Renard is the certainty, soon felt by the reader, that nothing is being put down in meanness or malice. The shadow of the small boy who had suffered bitterly because of the obsessions of his parents—his father's mutism, his mother's hypocrisy—always falls across the page. But Renard, in speaking difficult and shocking truths concerning Mme. Lepic (the name given to the mother of *Poil de Carotte* was carried over, in the *Journal*, to denote his own mother), does not hesitate to tell equally shocking truths about her red-headed son. Hard facts concerning family relationships were not usual in end-of-the-century writing. And Renard, in the *Journal*, presents the erotic elements in the son-mother relationship with extraordinary frankness—a frankness he shares with Stendhal (in *Henri Brulard*) before him, and with the Proust who is to come.

Truth about life, in Renard's view, had been distorted by literature. He applied himself to correct that distortion, not by the crass realism of Zola, but by an analysis based on sympathy, warmth, and tenderness. The peasants of his countryside were as important to him as his Parisian colleagues; they were his friends and his neighbors; even the dullest of his servants was not separated from his affection and attention. Animals were his familiars; he visited the Paris zoo regularly with enthusiastic interest, and he knew and felt for the wild and tame creatures of field and barnyard. The *Journal* celebrates the mystery, strangeness and beauty of bird and beast, seen without romantic coloring within their natural scene.

The final impression received from the *Journal* is one of delicacy backed up by power—power of character and power of intellect. Again and again those moments of insight appear which can only stem from absolute honesty of perception added to complete largeness of spirit. At these moments we understand why Renard's compatriots have not hesitated, some fifty years after his death, to name him among the masters.

The *Journal*, spanning twenty-four years, is a very long book. In its latest edition, the compact volume put out by the *Bibliothèque de la Pléiade* in 1960, it runs to 1267 pages. In making a selection that would place the writer and his preoccupations before the American reader, we have necessarily had to leave out, not only a large body of "writer's notes," but whole topics—such as Jules Renard's periods of service in the army; his accounts of the many literary banquets for which the period was famous; his espousal of the cause of Dreyfus (for he was an impassioned *dreyfusard*, and backed Zola with enthusiasm and indignation); his near-discipleship of the celebrated Socialist leader, Jean Jaurès; and his adoption—which appears more romantic than practical—of socialism. There are also a number of entries that are too topical to be of interest in this country and this time.

We have tried to establish, by the very things left out, a sort of continuity. In the texts we have chosen, the pleasures are many. There are, always, the single descriptive phrases, usually centered around an image that is at once poetic and piercingly exact; the insights into people and situations; the sketches of "his country" (one wishes he had done the same for Paris); the literary comment. Among the "threads" that run through the years we see the life of the writer as a man of letters, both in what it meant to him personally and in its aspect of worldly success—the *gloire* he always longed for but never quite achieved. We have his family life, especially the strange interrelationships of his parents and himself; we have the Paris friends, the big names—Sarah Bernhardt, Edmond Rostand, Lucien Guitry; and the country people to whom he always returned. As Léon Guichard wrote: "The *Journal* is a mine of inexhaustible riches." We have tried to extract its core.

—Louise Bogan

BEFORE 1887

A bronze bust of Jules Renard stands in the village of Chitry, some one hundred forty miles south of Paris. This was not, however, his birthplace. He was born, in 1864, at Châlons-sur-Mayenne, where his father was in charge of certain construction operations. But the elder Renard's place of origin was Chitry, and he brought his family back to it while his youngest son, on whose life and work the region was to exert so deep an influence, was still in his infancy. M. Renard *père* was shortly elected mayor of the village, apparently for life.

The future writer's childhood was a disaster. He had an older sister, Amélie, and an older brother, Maurice, mentioned at some length in the *Journal*. M. Renard, embittered by the death of a first-born daughter he had deeply loved, paid little attention to his other children. He was taciturn, violently *anticlérical*, rigidly honest. Mme. Renard was a bigot, and a compulsive talker and fibber. Shortly after the birth of her youngest son, her husband ceased speaking to her, and he never spoke to her again. Whether because of this coincidence or for some other reason, she came to vent all her frustration, resentment, and humiliation on this last child. Jules Renard later described his bitter childhood—from which he never entirely recovered—in a number of short pieces that were first published in different periodicals and then collected under the title *Poil de Carotte* ("Carrot-top"—he was a redhead). The bleak boarding school in Nevers to which he and his brother were sent became a haven to him, a place of refuge from his family.

When he was seventeen, his father, at the instance of his school principal, sent him to Paris to study rhetoric at the Lycée Charlemagne and to obtain his *baccalauréat*. He was to become a teacher.

By the time he was nineteen he had given up this idea. His father was sending him a small allowance. For the next few years—interrupted by a year's military service—he lived on that, supplemented rather painfully by odd clerking and tutoring jobs. He ghost-wrote a book on furniture. Meanwhile, he kept on writing short stories, only one of which was published—unpaid—at the time. He frequented literary cafés and certain newspaper milieux. All young men aspiring to a name in letters wrote poetry, and young Renard managed to publish, at his own expense, a collection of fairly banal verse, which he called *Les Roses*.

He was a country boy. His accent was not quite the accent of Paris, and his features were rough-hewn, but he was ambitious, and already wore the top hat and carried the elegant walking stick of the *boulevardier* he was to become. He must have had more than ordinary attractiveness, because, although he was penniless, his amie was a young actress of the Comédie Française, who tirelessly recited his poems in *salons*. (His inevitable break with her became, nine years later, the subject of his first and highly successful play, *Le Plaisir de Rompre*). He was also enthusiastically received in the homes of rich bourgeois reaching out for culture—a situation he later described in his novel *L'Ecornifleur*—"The Sponger" (1892).

He was desperately trying to find a stable situation, of almost any nature, and was even considering, much against his inclination, a post of schoolteacher in Algeria, when he met Mlle Marie Morneau. Her antecedents were undistinguished, but she was seventeen, pretty, and, by all accounts—not only Jules Renard's—gifted with a disposition almost Biblical in its selflessness. She, too, must have felt the attractiveness of the young Renard, for she not only married him, but brought him as part of her *dot* a narrow house on the Rue du Rocher, which became their Paris home, and a personal fortune of 300,000 francs.

Jules Renard continued for a while his part-time tutoring and other odd jobs, but he could from now on give himself over to finding his footing as an *homme de lettres*.

He began keeping the *Journal* in 1887, a year before he married. Where events of interest were left out of his entries–and at first the *Journal* was really a writer's notebook–we have indicated them in a note at the beginning of the year in which they occurred.

–Elizabeth Roget

1887

*It astounds us to come upon other egoists, as though we alone had
the right to be selfish, and be filled with eagerness to live.*

Jules Renard began his *Journal* this year, at the age of twenty-three.

The heavy sentence—as though weighted with electric fluids—of
Baudelaire.

A bird enveloped in mist, as though bringing with it fragments of
cloud torn with its beak.

Talent is a question of quantity. Talent does not write one page:
it writes three hundred. No novel exists which an ordinary intelligence could not conceive; there is no sentence, no matter how
lovely, that a beginner could not construct. What remains is to pick
up the pen, to rule the paper, patiently to fill it up. The strong do
not hesitate. They settle down, they sweat, they go on to the end.
They exhaust the ink, they use up the paper. This is the only difference between men of talent and cowards who will never make

a start. In literature, there are only oxen. The biggest ones are the geniuses—the ones who toll eighteen hours a day without tiring. Fame is a constant effort.

AUGUST

Sea foam. The tide seems to burst, like a muffled, distant explosion of which we should be seeing only the smoke.

SEPTEMBER

The true artist will write in, as it were, small leaps, on a hundred subjects that surge unawares into his mind. In this way, nothing is forced. Everything has an unwilled, natural charm. One does not provoke: one waits.

A scrupulous inexactness.

OCTOBER

Haughty, silent faces should not deceive us: these are the timid ones.

I have an almost incessant need of speaking evil of others; but no interest at all in doing evil to them.

It is a fascinating task to disentangle, in a young writer, the influences of the established ones. How hard we work before we help ourselves, quite simply, to our own originality!

How odd is the world of dreams! Thoughts, inner speech crowd and swarm—a little world hastening to live before the awakening that is its end, its particular death.

We often wish we could exchange our natural family for a literary one of our choice, in order that we might call the author of a moving page "brother."

On waking from a tender dream, we strive to go to sleep again in order to continue it, but we try in vain to seize its outlines as they disappear, like the folds of a beloved woman's dress, behind a curtain we cannot brush aside.

NOVEMBER

To lie watching one's mind, pen raised, ready to spear the smallest thought that may come out.

It astounds us to come upon other egoists, as though we alone had the right to be selfish, and be filled with eagerness to live.

Fresh, transparent air, in which the light looks washed, as though it had been dipped in clear water and then, like pieces of fine gauze, hung out to dry.

A style that's vertical, glittering, without seams.

Sometimes everything around me seems so diffuse, so tremulous, so little solid, that I imagine this world to be only the mirage of a world to come: its projection. We seem to be still far from the forest; and even though the great trees already cast their shadow over us, we still have a long journey to make before we walk under their branches.

It is in the heart of the city that one writes the most inspired pages about the country.

DECEMBER

Fingers knotty as a chicken's neck.

The chatting of the chairs, lined up before the guests arrive on a reception day.

Work thinks; laziness muses.

She has a very mean way of being kind.

In the goodness of things, the sea-shell is related to the stone.

1888

In order to do certain crazy things, it is necessary to behave like a coachman who has let go of the reins and fallen asleep.

JR marries Marie Morneau (Marinette in the *Journal*). He publishes, at his own expense, *Crime de Village*, a collection of short stories dedicated to his father.

AUGUST

In the woods, after lunch. We sit under a pine, above a rivulet running in the bark of a tree. A few bottles cooling in the water. Twigs dipping into it as though from thirst. The water rushes along, white with a few clear pools, so cold they almost hurt. My fat baby leans over my shoulder to see what I am writing. I kiss her, and it's delicious.

Nothing more boring than Gautier's portraits. The face is delineated feature by feature, with minute, encumbering details. Nothing of all this remains in the mind. Here is an error in this great writer, into which the modern school is careful not to fall. We depict with one precise word which makes an image, and no longer spend our time at microscopic surveys.

One morning, D. came to see me and said: "If you like, we'll buy two deal tables and each get a velvet skull cap, and then we'll start an Institution."

OCTOBER

Received a letter from my father that saddened me. Nothing about *Crime de Village;* not a word. Another vanity I shall have to get rid of.

He made a poem and began it thus: "Muse, tell me nothing! Keep quiet, Muse!"

NOVEMBER

Words are the small change of thought. Certain talkers pay us in ten-sou bits. Others, on the other hand, give out only gold pieces.

A thought written down is dead. It was alive. It lives no longer. It was a flower. Writing it down has made it artificial, that is to say, immutable.

Sometimes conversation dies out like a lamp. You turn up the wick. A few ideas bring out another gleam, but, decidedly, there is no oil left.

The poet should do more than dream: he should observe. I am convinced it is through observation that poetry must renew itself. It demands a transformation analogous to that which has taken place in the novel. Who would believe that an ancient mythology still oppresses us! What point is there to sing that the tree is inhabited by a faun? It is inhabited by itself. The tree lives: it is that fact which must be believed. A plant has a soul. A leaf is not what vain man thinks it is. We often talk of dead leaves, but we don't really believe that they die. What is the point of creating life outside of life? Fauns, you have had your day: the poet now wants to talk to the tree.

In order to do certain crazy things, it is necessary to behave like a coachman who has let go of the reins and fallen asleep.

How many people, after deciding to commit suicide, have been satisfied with tearing up their photograph!

1889

I can't get around this dilemma: I have a horror of troubles, but they whip me up, they make me talented. Peace and well-being, on the contrary, paralyze me. Either be a nobody, or everlastingly plagued.

JR's son, Jean-François, is born in Chitry. In November JR and nine others collaborate in founding the literary review, *Mercure de France*, originally named *La Pléiade*, the first issue of which appears December 25. Many of JR's short stories are to be published in this review.

JANUARY–Chitry

One thing has always astounded me: the universal admiration of the élite of the world of letters for Heinrich Heine. I must admit I can make nothing of this German who—a big mistake—tried to pose for French. His "Intermezzo" seems to me the work of a beginner attempting to do something poetic.

What must the life of a justice of the peace be like among the peasants, who pull him in all directions with their inexhaustible pigheadedness! They catch him even on the street. But the surest way, it seems, of getting at the truth with one of them is to say: "Will you take an oath on it?" This frightens the man. Awed, he hesitates. For all his slyness, he feels put off. He has a mind to lie, but would like to do it some other way. A Christ on the cross impresses him more than any amount of reasoning.

Once he has come home at night, the peasant possesses hardly more movement than a sloth. He is addicted to darkness, not only out of thrift, but out of preference. It rests his eyes, burnt by the sun. In the center of a circle of shadow, the stove roars through its little door, open like a red mouth.

A peasant must be twice sure of a fact before he will bet on it.

The mother has felt the first pains. The doctor is never called. One seldom has recourse to a midwife. Most often, a village woman presides at the lying-in. She knows herbs, and how to bind up a belly. While she performs, the others watch. It is an occasion for getting together. In order not to disturb the patient, they leave their wooden shoes near the door. Everything goes off well. The mother makes hardly more fuss than a cow.

The cradle must not be bought beforehand: in the first place, it is unlucky. And then, if there is a mishap, what will you do with it? Only the bassinet part comes from the basket-maker. The rockers come from the carpenter. They are made out of pine and properly trued, and he suggests that a strip of leather be attached underneath to muffle the sound. The wicker is painted to keep out the bedbugs. There is discussion over the color. The choice falls upon an "Easter-egg red," easily obtained from onions.

Once the child is born, it is entirely swaddled up, even to the arms, which are bound down. All you see is its head, purple and puffy. Babies have been seen wearing three bonnets.

The grandmother knits near the stove, in list slippers: wooden shoes are always kept at a good distance from the slippers. She sits with crossed legs. Attached to her free-hanging foot, and coming from the rocking cradle, is a string consisting of a piece of real string, the edging off a dress, and a piece of faded braid.

The scholar generalizes, the artist individualizes.

The blackbird, that minuscule crow.

Men of nature, as they are called, do not spend much time talking about nature.

Poets of the decadent school—the *décadents*—are reproached for their obscurity. This is not a valid criticism. What is there to understand in a line of verse? Absolutely nothing. Poetry is not an exercise from the Latin. I love Lamartine, but the music of his verse satisfies me. One does not gain much by peering under the words. There is little enough to find there. And one cannot demand of music that it have meaning, much meaning. Lamartine and the *décadents* agree on this point. They only consider form. The *décadents* make a little more fuss about it, that is all.

It should be forbidden, under penalty of a fine or even imprisonment, for a modern writer to borrow similes from mythology, to talk of harps, of lyres, of muses, of swans. Storks might pass.

The ideal of calm exists in a sitting cat.

FEBRUARY

One can well believe that the eyes of the newborn, those eyes that do not see and into which one finds it difficult to look, contain a little of the abyss from which they come.

A simple man, a man who has the courage to have a legible signature.

MARCH

The mother-in-law.[1]

"Yes, maman."

"In the first place, I am not your mother, and I have no use for your fine manners."

She would forget to set a place at table for her daughter-in-law, or would give her a dirty fork, or, when wiping the table, would purposely leave crumbs in front of her. In an extremity, she would heap all the crumbs in front of her. No means of annoyance was too small.

She could be heard saying: "Ever since this stranger has come, nothing goes right any more." And this stranger was the wife of her son. Her rage was further inflamed by the affection the father-in-law showed for the young woman. When she had to pass by her, she would draw herself together, pressing her arms against her sides, and flatten herself against the wall as though afraid of being dirtied. She would heave great sighs, and declare that if grief really killed she'd be dead. She would even spit to express her disgust.

Sometimes she would direct her attacks on the couple as a whole. "Maurice and Amélie, now, *there* are happy people, who get along well. Not like certain others, who only put on a show."

She would stop a village woman in the hallway, next to her daughter-in-law's door, and spin out her troubles. "What do you expect? They are young," the woman would say, while avidly enjoying the gossip. "Ah! they will not always be young!" the mother-in-law would go on. "Youth passes. I, too, used to kiss my husband, but that's all finished. Go on! Death takes us all. Just let me see them in ten years, or even before."

Let's be fair. She had her changes of mood, and they were very touching.

---

1 When he reread his *Journal* in 1906, JR added in the margin here: "It was this attitude toward my wife that made me write *Poil de Carotte*."

"My dear, my lovely, what can I do for you? Never mind what I say: I am as fond of you as I am of my own daughter. Here, let me fill your basin. Let me do the heavy work. Your hands are too white for that."

Suddenly, her face would turn nasty:

"Am I a maid-of-all-work?"

And, in her bedroom, she would separate the photographs of her children from those of her daughter-in-law, would leave her isolated, abandoned, no doubt sorely vexed.

To read two pages of Taine's *L'Intelligence* and then go and hunt dandelions—there's a dream, and that is my life for the time being. I attend the bedding down of the thrushes, the retiring of the woodcocks, the going to sleep of the woods. All this makes me stupid. Fortunately, two pages of Taine pull me out of the mud, and I am in full fantasy, above the world, furiously pursuing the study of my self, of its decomposition, of our annihilation.

APRIL

All I have read, all I have thought, all my forced paradoxes, my hatred of the conventional, my contempt for the commonplace, do not prevent me from turning soft on the first day of spring, from looking for violets under the hedges, among the turds and the scraps of decayed paper; from playing with the village youngsters, giving close attention to lizards and yellow-robed butterflies, bringing home a little blue flower to my wife. Everlasting contradiction. Continual effort to get beyond stupidity, and inevitable backsliding. Happily!

To have a horror of the bourgeois is bourgeois.

MAY

This morning, seated on a bundle of wood, in full sun, among the long leaves of lilies of the valley, while our eyes searched for their still-closed buds, we talked of nothing but death and what would happen if one of us were to go. The sun blinded us; our whole being was drenched with the desire to live, and we found it charming to talk of this inevitable death while it was still far away. Ah, those we leave behind! Fantec, his hat on his ear like a tough character, slept, smiled, sucked his bottle. A few men, placing the trunks of young oaks on two pitchforks stuck in the ground by their handles, swiftly divested them of their bark, a bark that was living and full of sap, like a skin, and that then shrank together in a last contraction.

The spider glides on an invisible thread as though it were swimming in the air.

The friendship of a talented man of letters would be a great benefaction. It is a pity that those whose good graces we yearn for are always dead.

Today, Marie Pierry's cow calved. Marie, in tears, said: "I can't watch that. I'm getting out of here."

Then she'd come back. "Oh, the poor dear! The poor dear! There! She is dead! I can see she is dead. She'll never pull out of it!"

The cow lowed and heaved sighs. Lexandre, pulling at the calf's legs, pouted his lips at her: "There, my beauty!" Father Castel presided: "Pull, children, pull!"

Everyone felt himself to be a mother, and when the cow, having produced her calf and drunk a bottle of sweetened wine, began licking the salt that had been sprinkled over the calf, everyone had tears in his eyes.

AUGUST

It's enough to throw you into despair: to read everything, and remember nothing! Because you do remember nothing. You may strain as much as you like: everything escapes. Here and there a few tatters remain, fragile as those puffs of smoke left over after a train has passed.

You can do what you like: until a certain age—I don't know what—there is no pleasure in talking to a woman you cannot imagine as a mistress.

SEPTEMBER–Paris

What do I want? La gloire! One man told me I had something in the belly. Another said I did things better and with less dirt than Maupassant . . . Still another . . . Is that supposed to be fame? No, men are too ugly, and I am as ugly as they. I do not like them; I can't care about what they think. Women, then? There was one, this evening, pretty, with a handsome bust, who said to me: "I read and reread *Crime de Village*." There is fame; I hold it in my hand. But this woman is a fool. She doesn't have an idea in her head. I should enjoy going to bed with her if she were deaf and dumb. If that were fame, there would be nothing left for me to do. And yet, proportions taken into account, that is all it is.

I can't get around this dilemma: I have a horror of troubles, but they whip me up, they make me talented. Peace and well-being, on the contrary, paralyze me. Either be a nobody, or everlastingly plagued. I must make a choice.

I prefer to be plagued. I am stating it.

I'll be properly annoyed when I am taken at my word.

I read novel upon novel, I stuff myself with them, inflate myself with them, I'm full up to my throat with them, in order that I may be disgusted with their commonplaces, their repetitions, their conventions, their systematic methods of procedure; and that I may do otherwise.

OCTOBER

In order to have an interesting head, he would carefully trim his hair every which way, with here and there a straight and protesting tuft to indicate the eccentricity of his thoughts and the boldness of his intentions.

You say, "I am vain," but you are especially vain of saying it.

Nothing is worse than the short stories of Balzac. The form is too small for him. Besides, when he had an *idea*, he made it into a novel.

This evening, memories are using my brain as a tambourine.

Papa has taken to wearing gloves like a young man. It is a vanity that has come to him late in life. If you were to ask him why, he would say that age is freezing the tips of his fingers.

NOVEMBER

We want to found a literary review. "Who will do the commentary?" each of us said. No one wanted to do the commentary. Someone suggested: "Let's take turns doing it."

In the end, it seemed that we all had some items of current comment in our pockets, ready to be delivered for the first issue . . .

Vallette, in his capacity of editor-publisher, embellishes his conversation with expressions such as: estimates, balances, incoming funds, accounts rendered.

Our scorn for money having been proclaimed loud and strong, we shall be enormously set up if the first issue brings in a profit of ten sous.

Last night, the 13th, first meeting of *La Pléiade* at the Café Français. There were some strange-looking characters. I thought we had done with long hair. It seemed as though I had come into a menagerie . . .

. . . [The legal standing of the periodical is discussed] . . . If there should be an attachment . . .

. . . Clearly, they had never owned anything subject to attachment. Still, an uneasiness had risen. The word was paralyzing. Each one saw himself seated on a bench in prison, surrounded by little baskets of food brought by friends.

. . . The danger of an attachment seemed to have been removed. Vallette, editor-in-chief, consulted a scrap of paper:

"First the name. Are we keeping the name of *La Pléiade*?"

I didn't dare say it, but I found this starry title a little old-fashioned. Why not Scorpio or the Big Dipper? And groups of poets had already used that name—under Ptolemy Philadelphus, under Henry III and under Louis XIII. Nevertheless, the name was adopted.

And the color of the cover?

"Butter yellow." "Mat white." "Apple green." "No! Like a horse I saw—dappled gray chestnut. No! No!"

Vallette didn't quite remember the horse he had seen.

"The color of tobacco with milk poured over it."

"Shall we make the experiment?"

A bowl of milk was brought, but no one offered his tobacco to be wasted.

We began to go through the series of colors, but couldn't find the right words. Verlaine should have been there. Without him we tried to make do with gestures, spread fingers, impressionistic attitudes, suspended movements, forefingers stabbing the air.

"And you, Renard?"

"Oh, I don't care."

I feigned indifference, but in truth I adore the green of certain magazines after they have been washed by the weather in the kiosques.

"And you, Court?"

"I side with the majority."

"Everybody is siding with the majority. What is the majority for?"

It was concentrating on mauve. Mauve curtains are so pretty! And then the word rhymes with alcove, and the association of ideas brought a humid gleam to the eye of Aurier: perhaps he knows an elegant great lady.

Vallette began again:

"On the back cover we will put (won't we?) the titles of our published works."

No one said a word.

"And of works to be published."

Everyone tried to speak. Aurier: "*Le Vieux*;" Vallette: "*Babylas*." Dumur: "*Albert*." And the list grew longer, full of titles as though it were descended from the Crusades.

"And you, Renard?"

"I have no titles. But, as for copy, I have a lot of that!"

I seemed to imply that they had none. They looked at me side-wise.

"Now about the format," said Vallette. "Perhaps we should have started with that."

"Don't care." "Don't give a damn–"

"Excuse me," said Aurier. "We need air, and margins, wide margins. The text must be able to move about the paper."

"Yes, but that has to be paid for." "Oh!" "I request the format in 18vo so it will fit my bookcase . . ."

. . . "Now let's take a look at the contents. Everybody must contribute to the first issue."

"We'll be like sardines in a can."

The review was cut up into slices.

"I'll take ten. Yes, ten. I'll pay thirty francs for them."

We finally got lined up like passengers in a stage-coach. I was forgiven for not having any poetry to offer, because they were all contributing poetry.

"A frontispiece and tail-pieces, of course."

"Oh, yes, many tail-pieces to keep the poems separate, because they will follow upon each other's heels like customers at a box-office who are afraid they won't get in. And suppose they should become mixed up! . . ."

Vallette will write an article on *La Pléiade*. This approximately will be its gist: there are three reasons for founding a literary review. 1. To make money. We do not wish to make money—

We looked at each other. Who, here, would say that he wished to make money? No one. A happy situation.

"Are we by chance *décadents*?"

"No! Not with Baju. He is a schoolteacher, you know."

"Too bad! The god Verlaine will not seat us on his right hand."

"Do we plan on clarity?"

"Yes, clarity." "Entire clarity." "Oh! entire clarity. Let's not exaggerate. Let's say chiaroscuro."

"Bring only the top of your baskets," Vallette said.

Samain, a young man of distinguished aspect, wearing stylish gloves, who so far had said nothing, being entirely taken up with sketching a fat woman's bottom on the table, remarked:

"And we will give what's underneath to *Le Figaro*."

"Don't knock *Le Figaro*. Aurier belongs to it."

"So does Randon." . . .

Unhappily, the question of monetary contributions came up. Vallette announced that he would put them down as they were called, but in pencil, so they could be erased at the first sign of regret. Renard, 30 francs; Dumur, 20; Vallette, 10; Raynaud, 10; Court, 5. It went on diminishing like a lizard's tail. I wondered if it would end by someone contributing a button. Justly proud, by virtue of my 30 francs, I promptly conceived a high opinion of myself and of the Universe, and disdainfully neglected to say anything that might crush, under a pile of guarantees, the suspicions as to my solvency that must certainly have been springing up in the hearts of these men.

It was decided that we would meet the first and the last Friday of each month in some café on the decline, "to give it a boost". It was decided that we would then pay two contributions at a time, because a review should be able to say "I exist", and that is not as easy as Descartes thought.

The glasses were empty. Three lumps of sugar remained in a saucer. Aurier picked them up between his thumb and forefinger and offered them from afar. Heads moved from side to side. He did not insist, but placed them in the pocket of his Prince Albert. "It's for my rabbits," he said, parodying a joke by Taupin. For tomorrow's breakfast, most likely.

From eleven o'clock until midnight, in silence, all braced themselves for the final moment. There was good reason: who would pick up the check? Surmises, sly and wordless, walked like spiders under the benches. The thirty-franc capitalist owed himself the gesture, but preferred to remain owing it. One by one, the tarts left, this one alone, that one fiercely hanging onto the arm or the coattails of a man afflicted with the itch. The waiters began to make free with the property of the establishment, sitting on the tables and chairs. The cashier started adding up her till, and we were made painfully aware of the loud clinking of silver coins.

Noticing this, one of us, M. Samain, called a waiter and said: "How much?"

"All the coffees?"

"No: one."

"Forty centimes, monsieur."

He gave him fifty centimes and stood up. Each man for himself and two sons for the waiter. Now there was a *man*!

[Quoted from Rivarol] "His ideas resemble the pile of glass panes in a glazier's basket: separately clear, opaque when together."

I am fond of people in the degree to which they furnish me with notes.

DECEMBER

That poignant sensation which makes you take hold of a sentence as though it were a weapon.

1890

*I'm intelligent, more intelligent than many others.
This is obvious, since I can read* The Temptation of Saint
Anthony *without falling asleep. But this intelligence is like
water running, unknown, unused, in some region where no one
has yet built a mill. Yes, that is it: I have not yet found my mill.
Shall I ever find it?*

This year marks JR's true literary debut. He publishes many short pieces, moves in the circle of letters. In October, his stories appear in a collection, *Sourires Pincés*, which provokes many notices and articles. However, his novel, *Les Cloportes*, does not find a publisher (it was published posthumously in 1919).

JANUARY

You can be a poet and still wear your hair short.
    You can be a poet and pay your rent.
    Even though you are a poet, you can sleep with your wife.
    And a poet may even, at times, write proper French.

One should operate by dissociation, and not by association, of ideas. An association is almost always commonplace. Dissociation decomposes, and uncovers latent affinities.

The bourgeois are the others.

FEBRUARY

This man of genius is an eagle stupid as a goose.

Rod is still making a distinction between exterior observation and interior observation or intuitivism. As though psychology had not long ago proven that all observation is interior!

Avid to know everything, to be au courant, I have come to be fond of very short books, easy to read, printed in large type with many white spaces, so that I may toss them into my bookcase as quickly as possible and pass on to others.

One enters a book as one enters a railway carriage, with glances to the rear, hesitations, and a disinclination to change one's place and one's ideas. Where will the journey take us? What will the book turn out to be?

The annoyance of having to pass in front of a bench on which people are sitting. Because, in truth, sitting on a bench places a man at a great advantage. He can look people over, laugh if he pleases, think his thoughts. He knows that the passers-by can do nothing of the kind; they can neither stop, nor look, nor, in their turn, laugh.

Look for the ridiculous in everything and you will find it.

The questing, circular look with which an actor, even in the midst of his gravest preoccupations, will seek to assure himself that people are looking at him and that he has been recognized.

The critic enjoys the right to disown his articles one after another, and his duty is to have no convictions of any kind.

MARCH

Fantec is walking. He takes a dozen steps all by himself, falls on his bottom and begins to laugh, and runs as soon as he is within reach of his mother's knees.

I am going through a nasty phase. All books disgust me. I do nothing. I notice more than ever that I am of no use. I feel that I shall not get anywhere; and these lines that I am writing seem to rue childish, ridiculous, and, especially, entirely useless. How to get out of here? I have one expedient: hypocrisy. I remain locked up for hours, and people think I am working. Some may be sorry for me, others admire me, and I am bored, and I yawn, my eye full of jaundiced reflections from the yellow of my bookcase. I have a wife who is a strong and gentle creature full of life, a baby who could take prizes in a contest, and I have no strength to enjoy all that. I know that this mood will pass. I shall have hopes again, and new braveries, and will make brand-new efforts. If only these confessions were of some use to me! If later I could become a great psychologist, as great as M. Bourget! But I do not believe that I possess enough power. I shall die before my time, or else become a drunkard of day-dreams. Better to break stones, plow fields. And shall I spend my life saying: Better turn to something else? Why this seesawing of our soul, this coming and going of our enthusiasms? Our hopes are like the waves of the sea: when they withdraw, they leave uncovered a mess of sickening objects, foul shells and crabs, stinking moral crabs forgotten on this beach, that now drag themselves sideways to catch up with the sea. How sterile is the life of a writer who doesn't get there! Goodness, I'm intelligent, more intelligent than many others. This is obvious, since I can read *The Temptation of Saint Anthony* without falling asleep. But this intelligence is like water running, unknown, unused, in some region where no one has as yet built a mill. Yes, that is it: I have not yet found my mill. Shall I ever find it?

That scoffer Dubus was in a state of emotion yesterday, and almost turning pale, because someone had told him that some newspaper had printed something about him.

Never having as yet observed anything, he loved the grand and the emphatic.

APRIL

A tree with a curving trunk seemed to want to go down on its knees.

A senseless wind pushing before it, with an extraordinary expenditure of breath, two or three little white clouds in the shape of rabbits.

MAY–At the seashore (Barfleur)

Our little Fantec is diverting to watch. He has cheeks remarkably like buttocks and a complexion like a copper piece. But he is terrified of the crabs that walk sideways and the lobsters with their blindmen's gropings. We put a little crayfish in the pocket of his pinafore, whereupon he placed his hands behind his back like Napoleon after Moscow, and stood that way a good half-hour, possessed by I know not what thoughts, walking backwards now and then, and pretty perplexed by this toy that moved on his stomach. This might be a way of making him behave which we had not thought of.

What the Goncourts lack, perhaps, is the art of making their words, their interesting quirks of language stand out, of setting them in the window so that the passer-by will stop and take notice. You are aware of their wit–and it is wit of the rarest kind–only after the second or third reading. But a proper man does not read the same thing through twice.

Realism! Realism! Give me a fine reality and I will model myself on it.

JUNE

I have built such beautiful castles that I would be satisfied with their ruins.

Reread *Le Curé de Village* [Balzac]. The death of Mme. Graslin is a very beautiful thing. However, I believe that this kind of novel is dead, at least for men of great talent. It creates an illusion. It produces a terrific effect, but the effect does not last, and then one is inclined to smile. . . . I believe that really gifted writers will soon no longer be able to write that kind of book.

In his *Paysans*, Balzac makes the peasant loquacious: I believe that he is not talkative at all. Balzac has too much genius: he even gives some to his peasants.

When I make a joke, I watch the maid out of the corner of my eye to see if she is laughing.

The regret of not being on intimate terms with a writer you admire makes you critical of him.

A painter is a man who wears a beret.

If you are in a mood to laugh, you will find me witty.

Ah! our vanity! In *Le Roquet*, I find my article, "Art for Money," mercilessly emasculated. All morning, I have felt as though penknives were jabbing my flesh.

JULY

An exotic plant opening like a fan of razors.

AUGUST

Mérimée may be the writer who will last longest. He makes less use than any other of the image, that prime cause of the aging of a style. Posterity will belong to dry, constipated writers.

SEPTEMBER

Vallette defined Flaubert: perfection in talent, but in talent only.

Amazing, how fond writers can be of each other while running each other down!

We are ignorant of the Beyond because this ignorance is the condition *sine qua non* of our own life. Just as ice cannot know fire except by melting, by vanishing.

DECEMBER

Met Alphonse Daudet this morning. He got to his feet, looked at me in the light, and said: "I recognize Poil de Carotte." A fine head, quite like the one we see in the shop windows, the beard with a sprinkling of salt. A Provençal very much gentled down, old, a little crippled, walking with the help of a cane with a rubber tip. He complimented me very highly. I did not know how I should answer. Should I say, "Monsieur", or "Cher Maître"? He talked to us a bit about everything, without show of wit, but with breadth, good sense.

1891

[André Gide] is clean-shaven, has a cold in the nose and throat, an exaggerated jaw, eyes between two welts. He is in love with Oscar Wilde, whose photograph I perceive on the mantel: a fleshy gentleman, very refined, also clean-shaven, who has recently been discovered.

JANUARY

At eleven-thirty last night, the door-bell rings. It is M. Marcel Schwob, asking me, through the door, for "a story for *L'Echo de Paris.*" By the light of two candles, I see a round face, a balding head. We search through my papers, in vain.

He wanted to take me to the office of *L'Echo de Paris* on the spot, as I was, with bare feet and in my nightshirt.

Anyway, a fine chance missed!

FEBRUARY

The style of [J.K.] Huysmans is like a hard brush, which scratches, and in which there are some very big, very coarse bristles.

This morning, had a good conversation, of an hour and a half, with Alphonse Daudet. He seemed to be in less pain, walked almost naturally, was gay. [Edmond de] Goncourt had said to him: "Tell *Sourires Pincés* that I am not forgetting him, that I'll write as soon as I have finished *La Fille d'Elisa.*" Goncourt is not above the petty torments of the literary life. A spiteful article in *Le Figaro* offended him deeply; he was upset for a long time . . .

[Daudet:] "You will get there, Renard. I am sure of it, and you will make money, but to do that you will now and then have to give yourself a kick in the pants . . .

"The Symbolists, what poor, absurd creatures! Don't talk about them! There is nothing abstruse. Every man of talent gets there, and I fanatically believe that all work has its wages. Why don't you come on Thursdays . . ."

I warmly shook his hand and said: "Cher Maître, you have made me feel better for a long time."

MARCH

Yesterday, at Daudet's: Goncourt, Rosny, Carrière, Geffroy, M. and Mme. Toudouze, M. and Mine. Rodenbach. Why did I leave disgusted? No doubt I had imagined that Goncourt was not a man. Must the old be possessed of all the pettinesses of the young? How they worked over that poor Zola . . .

Goncourt looks like a fat retired army man. I saw no wit in him: that will have to wait for another time. Until that second impression, all he has is the repetitiousness I find so intolerable in the works of the Goncourts . . .

A bad day, yesterday. At *L'Echo de Paris* they found my story *Le Navet Sculpté* [The Carved Turnip] too subtle; and I found our great men too coarse.

Today, went to Daudet's, then we went to see Rodin, then Goncourt. Very unluckily, I seem to have made Goncourt dislike me. Why didn't I blindly compliment him on his books, which I haven't read! Cold greeting, the barest civilities, no sort of invitation, not a word from his wife concerning my wife and child. My boy, you must have properly put your foot in it. Ah, the way life steps on one's toes! . . .

At Rodin's, a revelation, an enchantment: the "Door of Hell," and that little thing, no bigger than my hand, that is called "The Eternal Idol;" a man, vanquished, his arms behind his back, kisses a woman under the breasts, his lips against her skin, and the woman seems overcome with sadness. I cannot easily detach myself from that . . .

In the court, blocks of marble wait to be given life; they are strange, in their shapes and, it would seem, in their desire to live. It is funny: I play the man who has discovered Rodin.

Rodin, this sculptor of voluptuous pain, who looks like a pastor, naïvely asks Daudet what he should call his overwhelming creations. He fastens upon simple little names taken, for example, from mythology . . .

Goncourt [to me]:

"You don't smoke?"

"No!"

"Oh! you want to have a style of your own."

In Rodin's atelier, it seemed as though my eyes suddenly burst open. Until now sculpture interested me like work done on turnips.

To write in the manner that Rodin sculpts.

When someone shows me a drawing, I look at it just long enough to prepare a comment.

Discussion between Raynaud and myself on the subject of Mallarmé. I say: "It is stupid." He says: "It is marvelous." And that resembles all literary discussions.

Something terrible may be about to happen here. Today the word *croup* was uttered by a celebrity with a pince-nez, who charges 40 francs a visit. Afterwards we no longer knew what he had said. Marinette is weeping . . . We are drunk with fear.

We are confused on pharynx and larynx.

M. and Mme. Oury and their baby come to call.

"Our child is threatened with the croup."

"Oh, it won't be anything!"

They tumble down the stairs, pale with terror, waving their arms and repeating: "It will be nothing! It will be nothing!"

Last night, Schwob stayed until two o'clock in the morning. With delicate fingers, he seemed to be taking my brain, turning it over and exposing it to the light of day. He talked of Aeschylus and compared him to Rodin . . .

One moment, the lamp went out. I lighted the candles on the piano. The face of Marcel Schwob was in shadow.

I feel that this man will have an enormous influence on me.

Balzac is perhaps the only one who had the right to write badly.

APRIL

Style is to forget all styles.

Daudet, in fine fettle, tells us of the embarkations of Gauguin, who would like to go to Tahiti in order to find nobody there, and who never goes. So that his best friends are finally saying to him: "You must leave, my dear fellow, you must leave."

The critic is a botanist. I am a gardener.

Last night, at Daudet's . . .

Goncourt talks, with a good nature that (why?) appears to me false, of the insignificant sale of his books . . .

Rosny carries on and on about his *bête noire*, Huysmans. I hear: "In order to vomit one's times, you would have to have eaten them first. Everyone is a rebel, these days."

Upon which Daudet remarks: "I refused to become a member of the Academy, and yet nobody takes me for a rebel. Why is that?"

A clean-shaven gent speaks to me interminably about my book. How insufferable I should find him if he talked about anything else!

Schwob says: "It is perhaps in the Bible that one might find novel literary procedures and the art of leaving things in their places."

MAY

Rodin, that good man, tells us naïvely: "I studied with Barye, but I did not understand him. I thought he had too much simplicity to be a great artist."

To seize the fleeing idea by the scruff of the neck and rub its nose on the paper.

Yesterday, saw the Monet exhibition. Those hayricks with blue shadows, those fields colored like a checkered handkerchief.

Never to be satisfied: all of art is there.

AUGUST

My mis-shapen head cracks through all the clichés.

OCTOBER

Perhaps people with a very good memory cannot have general ideas.

Yesterday, dinner at Descaves' with Huysmans, Bonnetain.

Huysmans, of course, entirely different from what I had imagined. Graying, a pointed beard, hard, clear-cut features. One could recognize him by his hatred for Rosny.

[He says to me] "Carrot, cut out carrot. You don't want it. Carrot is not a word used in high society. . . ."

My friends wait for me at the novel, as they might wait at a street corner.

NOVEMBER

Amazing, how much better all these literary celebrities look in caricature!

Yesterday, collected my first sou for my writing. At such a moment, a sou is as handsome as 500,000 francs.

[Catulle] Mendès: "One day I was having dinner at Cladel's [Léon Cladel, novelist]. He was amusing himself uncovering the backside of his little boy and setting him on the soup tureen. It warmed the kid's bottom, made Cladel laugh, and gave us an appetite."

DECEMBER

How vain is an idea! Without the sentence, I'd retire.

I very humbly confess my pride.

When you come out of the Théâtre d'Art, you feel like addressing your wife as the beloved of your soul, and the maid as daughter of Jerusalem . . .

Many people talk to me about my novel, about to appear, in order not to have to say anything after it will have appeared.

It is pretty unfortunate that our taste improves while our talent stands still.

At Schwob's, met André Gide, the author of *Les Cahiers d'André Walter*. Schwob introduces me as someone insufferably pig-headed.

"And if you are not," says Gide in a reedy voice, "you look it."

He is clean-shaven, has a cold in the nose and throat, an exaggerated jaw, eyes between two welts. He is in love with Oscar Wilde, whose photograph I perceive on the mantel: a fleshy gentleman, very refined, also clean-shaven, who has recently been discovered.

Today, having collected 215 francs at the office of *Gil-Blas*, I smile at the bookkeeper, at the cashiers, I am exquisite with everyone. Man is not half a fool.

1892

At the café, [Verlaine] is addressed as "Maître" and "cher Maître," but he is worried, and wants to know what they did with his hat. He looks like a drunken god. All that is left of him is our cult. Above clothes in ruins—a yellow tie, an overcoat that must stick to his flesh in several places—a head out of building stone in process of demolition.

JANUARY

[At the office of *L'Echo de Paris*] "I will write an article on *L'Ecornifleur*," says Schwob, "Long or short, no matter, in which I'll prove that you are a mystic."

"You'll have a hard time," say I.

Schwob to dinner.

"Daudet told us this. He was having dinner at Victor Hugo's. The great poet of course presided, but in isolation, at one end of the table. He was almost deaf, and no one spoke to him, the guests gradually drawing away, toward youth, toward Jeanne and Georges [his adult grandchildren]. He had been practically forgotten, when suddenly, at the end of the meal, the voice of the great man with the bristling beard was heard—a deep voice, coming from afar: "I didn't get any cake!"

Schwob told us further:
"Baudelaire, in a beer tavern, declared: 'There's a smell of destruction here.' 'Why, no,' he was told, 'There's a smell of sauerkraut, and of slightly warm woman.' But Baudelaire repeated with violence: 'I tell you it smells of destruction!'"

Those evenings at Daudet's! About the most interesting things you hear: Goncourt: "Maupassant knows his craft. He turns out a very good Norman peasants' story . . . But he isn't a great writer; not what *we* would call an artist."
Who are *we*? He repeats: "He is not an artist," and looks around to see if anyone will protest. No one does.
Daudet: "What killed him was wanting to compete with others: He would say to himself: Barrès has published a book this year, Bourget and Zola have published, but I haven't published anything yet. That is what killed him . . ."
Goncourt's hand has the softness of a damp featherbed.

Oh, the great days of petty vexations! The buttonhook will not catch a single button; my suspenders turn into corkscrews in my back; and those rags are my socks. My eyes turn back what they see, and all my senses hurt. The only pleasure I have left is to talk harshly to Marinette, who hardly dares move for fear of irritating me. Where is the shoe-horn? As for my tie, I have never, in all my life, seen anything as grotesque-looking as that tie. And I am crushed by the weight of my clothes.

Met Goncourt in Ollendorf's office [JR's publisher]. His face shows fatigue, as though it were eaten by time. When he speaks, he pretends to address himself only to Schwob. He talks of his *Journal*, which is making enemies for himself, and mostly so when he is trying to be pleasant. But this is finished: the remaining part will appear after his death, in thirty years; let's say twenty.

I could stand a man who would say, "Look at my beautiful blond beard!" But I cannot abide the man who says, "I am an honorable man." For I know he is guilty of at least one impropriety a day, just as I am.

This journal of mine will offend many people. It has offended even me . . . I do not feel that I have been sincere; I tried too hard to have succeeded.

My friends will recognize themselves in it. I think I have spoken sufficiently ill of them to make them feel flattered.
    You are told: "Look at life!" I have looked at people living.

We are all poor fools (of course I am speaking of myself), incapable of being either good or bad for two consecutive hours.

FEBRUARY

He keeps on his hat out of fear of colds, removes it often out of courtesy, and quickly puts it on again out of prudence.

When he looked at himself in a mirror, he was always tempted to wipe the glass.

MARCH

Yesterday, dinner at *La Plume*. Intelligent faces of intelligent men are rare. A studied ugliness, like the handles of walking canes. The frightful Verlaine: a dismal Socrates and a soiled Diogenes; part dog, part hyena. All of a tremble, he lets himself fall on a chair that someone carefully moves into place behind him. Oh, that laugh through the nose—a nose as precise as an elephant's trunk—through the eyebrows and the forehead!

When Verlaine came in, a gent who a few minutes later was to prove himself a fool cried out:

"Hail to genius! I don't know him, but hail to genius!" And he clapped his hands.

The counsel for *La Plume* exclaimed:

"The proof that he has genius is that he doesn't give a damn about it!"

Then a few cold meats were brought to Verlaine, who kept on brooding.

At the café, he is addressed as "Maître" and "cher Maître," but he is worried, and wants to know what they did with his hat. He looks like a drunken god. All that is left of him is our cult. Above clothes in ruins—a yellow tie, an overcoat that must stick to his flesh in several places—a head out of building stone in process of demolition . . .

Deschamps mentions my name. Immediately, Scholl stands up, comes over to me, and, after a flow of compliments, tells me:

"Yesterday, I was in the dressing-room of Felicia Mallet [an actress]. She was reading your book. She said to me: 'Read that! It's wonderful!' I quite concur. Your title has put a word back into circulation. Do you know that I had to look it up in the dictionary?"

Verlaine's eyes, as though crushed under the stone block of his forehead.

"There is in Verlaine," says Schwob, "an honorable man, a citizen, a patriot, who believes in the usefulness of his life, who says: 'I have added to the glory of France,' and who would like to be given the Legion of Honor."

He would like to have words eat out of his hand.

It is rather odd that I can't read two pages of Thackeray without yawning, when my humour is supposed to resemble his.

APRIL

Oscar Wilde next to me at lunch. He has the oddity of being an Englishman. He gives you a cigarette, but he selects it himself. He does not walk around a table, he moves a table out of the way. His face is kneaded with tiny red worms, and he has long teeth, containing caves. He is enormous, and he carries an enormous cane.

MAY

Yesterday, at Saint-Cloud, couples lay in each other's arms. Other couples would look at them, laugh, and settle down a little farther on. In the midst of this imposing setting, on one of the grassy flights of steps going to the terrace that faces the ruins, a young couple—a curly-headed little woman, a deft young man—were making love to each other in gestures. A hundred-and-fifty people strung out on the steps were catching fire watching them, fine-looking gentlemen were buttoning up their overcoats, while young girls, serious and a little pale, surveyed the sport.

The spectacle drained the strength out of our legs, so that we were compelled to lie down on the grass and hunt for crickets' holes. In the distance, Paris raised her buildings like playing dice. Well-pruned trees lost themselves in the sky. The young man and young woman became aware of the attention they were attracting, but, undisturbed, continued to play . . .

A woman raised small opera glasses and used them as though she were at the theatre. And if you turned your head, you beheld ruins within which so many nights of love had so quickly passed . . .

We said: "It's the spring! It's the spring!" And, to make fun of our melancholy: "No! The government paid this couple, to attract the public. We ought to take advantage of this moment of love, because tomorrow we'll again be serious and reserved." Mothers of the girls who were being teased sulked and showed annoyance at not being able to take part in their excursions.

It was chance tenderness, false tenderness. Never had we missed women to such a degree. In order to divert our minds we tried to climb to the top of the terrace on one foot, but our flaccid legs gave way under us, and we touched the ground.

We held blades of grass in our teeth.

In art, never do as others do; in morals, act like everybody else.

JUNE

I have made enemies because I am unable to discover talent in all those who tell me I am full of it.

JULY

At twenty, one thinks profoundly and badly.

He is deaf in the left ear: he does not hear on the side of the heart.

AUGUST

There is in my heart something like the reflection of a beautiful dream that I no longer remember.

Just suppose him dead for an instant, and see if he is without talent!

A fly alighting on the sheet of white paper was excuse enough for him to give himself the right to be idle. He did not write, for fear of disturbing the fly.

SEPTEMBER

Every time the wind blows down the chimney, Poil de Carotte remembers his childhood.

The fear of boredom is the only excuse for working.

To be a boy, and to play alone, in full sunlight, in the square of a little town.

He had a fear of working, and was annoyed because he did not work.

He wept cats and dogs.

OCTOBER

M. Ernest Renan having died, a few young men are anxiously asking what is to become of us. We can do without faith. I should like to see a man suffering from doubt as he would suffer from an infected finger, and screaming with rage. Then I shall believe in moral suffering.

I, too, went to call on Renan.

Renan is an example of what can be done without style.

Verlaine. Ah yes! a particularly muddy Socrates. Arrives smelling of absinthe. Vanier gives him five francs, against a receipt, and Verlaine stands there, mumbles, talks by means of gestures, by drawing his brows together, with the folds of his scalp, his poor wisps of hair, and his mouth in which wild boars could live, and his hat and tie out of a garbage can. Talks of Racine, of Corneille "whose stock is going down." He says:

"I have talent, genius …"

. . . He smiles at me, talks about his elegies, of Victor Hugo, of Tennyson, a great poet, and says:

"I write poetry man to man. I talk in verse. Elegies are beautiful, simple. They have no form. I no longer want form, I despise it. If I wanted to write a sonnet, I would write two."

Says to me:

"Monsieur is rich?"

Takes off his hat and bows to the ground, offers to walk with me to the corner, looks at his absinthe with speaking eyes, looks at it as though it were a lake of colors, and, when I pay, tells me:

"I'm poor today. I'll have money tomorrow."

He holds Vanier's five-franc piece firmly in his palm and says, like a small child:

"I'm going to be good, work. My little woman will no doubt come and kiss me. I don't care if I live in filth, so long as she can eat lobster."

He mumbles around, disgusts, hangs on, stamps in a sickly way to make sure he's on his feet, is fond of Vanier.

"They shouldn't try to turn me against him. He doesn't make much money on me!"

As soon as Vanier's back is turned, he shakes his fist:

"Swine of a publisher! I am Vanier's milk-teat."

Yesterday, Schwob was full of subtle smiles. We were arguing. He would smile at my wife as though to say: "What a stubborn fellow! Isn't he ridiculous!" I had a strong desire to put my foot in his face, because Marinette, politely, was smiling too.

One gets fed up with writing well.

When I saw my village again, its houses seemed so small that I was about to write my name with my finger on the snow of their roofs.

NOVEMBER

He who is afraid of pronouncing English words.

The flutter of Schwob's eyelids when he is lying.

Every now and then he had to skim off his seething thoughts.

DECEMBER

The hours when we should like to write nothing but music.

The green moons of winter.

1893

*Whenever I have talked to anyone at too great length,
I am like a man who has drunk too much, and, ashamed,
doesn't know where to put himself.*

JR publishes two collections of short stories—*Cocquecigrues* and *La Lanterne*.

JANUARY

When he praises anyone, he feels that he is slightly disparaging himself.

Remembrances of childhood like drawings done with a match.

A thin old professor who looked like a cobra.

To write about a friend is to break with him.

He spent his entire life on a jump-seat.

My pen makes a noise like a goose eating grass.

FEBRUARY

I like Maupassant because he seems to be writing for me, not for himself. He seldom goes in for confessions. He does not say: "Here is my heart," or "Truth comes out of my well." His books either entertain or bore. You close them without anxiously asking yourself: "Is this great, middling, or small art?" The stormy, excitable esthetes scorn his name, because it gives back no echoes.

It is possible that, having once read Maupassant in his entirety, you would not want to read him again.

But those who wish to be reread will not even be read in the first place.

MARCH

Nulla dies sine linea. And he wrote a line a day, no more.

But why does Claudel write *Tête d'Or* and *la Ville* in one manner, while his compositions to obtain the post of vice-consul in New York are done in another? An artist must be the same when he prays and when he eats.

He wore his crown of laurels on his ear.

APRIL

It is now the fashion, when one has completed someone's portrait in the blackest of strokes, to add:

"But he is very nice."

The more one reads, the less one imitates.

When I want to be a man of action, I read the life of Balzac, by Théophile Gautier. This satisfies me. For an hour, I am possessed by the fever, the desire of greatness. I am a fiery horse, and nothing can withstand my impetuous forward dash. Then I calm down, I forget the whole thing, and I've been a man of action as well as the next one.

Yes, I know. All great men were unknown at first. But I am not a great man, and I should be just as pleased to be known now.

One should work only in the evening, when one is filled with the stimulation of the entire day.

MAY

A gentle eye, a gentle voice, a soft skin; scratching his fingers, rubbing his ring, Veber, a young man of seventeen, calmly compared for us the real world with the unreal; and it seemed as though he had just left Plato, having met him under the arcades of the Odéon while browsing over books; and that, under the horse-chestnuts of the Luxembourg gardens, the master had then for his benefit set forth his latest theories.

I am moved by nature because, when I look at her, I need not worry about looking stupid.

Perhaps the world was created only that evil might be fulfilled. If we went with the movement instead of counter to it, something good would follow.

As I was mildly joshing d'Esparbès, he said:
   "To me, you are the foremost writer of our time."
   I believed him at once, and regretted my pleasantries.

Young men of twenty have said to me:
   "You are better than La Fontaine."
   When I repeat this, I add:
   "They are young and ingenuous, but extraordinarily intelligent for their age."

To spend one's life judging oneself is very entertaining, and, on the whole, not very difficult.

Daudet says to me:
"You have made amazing progress in the French language. Now, each one of your words is chiseled out."

The exhausting torture of saying no for an hour to a gentleman who wants you to say yes.

"What is referred to as the genius of Claudel," says Bernard Lazare, "is nothing but aphasia. With a great deal of force, he emits sounds some of which mean something while the others are unintelligible. He fills our ears with an uproar which, here and there, makes a certain sense. A man of genius should know how to compose. Otherwise, a man of talent would be better."
As an exaggeration, this is not exaggerated.

If the word *arse* appears in a sentence, even in a sublime sentence, the public will hear only that one word.

JUNE

The inert egoism that is called the country.

And the brook murmurs without pause against the stones that try to prevent it from flowing.

The old man, finding in a cupboard the expensive toys he was not allowed to play with as a child. With softened eyes and a sad smile, he looks at them, but they were forbidden to him for so long that, even now, he doesn't dare touch them.

JULY

François Coppée calls me his "dear boy." It is very nice of him, but it makes us sound like a couple of drunks.

The little man who answers "Five centimes" instead of "A sou," when you ask the price of a bunch of flowers, is already possessed of literary vanity.

SEPTEMBER

How describe the delicate thing that happens when a brilliant insect alights on a flower? Words, with their weight, fall upon the picture like birds of prey.

I am never bored anywhere: being bored is an insult to oneself.

If you thought highly of your family, you would want to please them; and if you tried to please them, that would be the end of you.

A village where only the trees are capable of emotion.

The clouds, their bellies swollen with rain, crawl over the woods like black spiders.

Style means the right word. The rest matters little.

There would seem to be a lot of needles between us. We keep getting pricked. It is not painful, but, still, there is blood.

Critics, who always speak about others and about whom no one speaks, are entitled to forbearance.

OCTOBER

Your sole preoccupation is to be sincere. But don't you find this constant search for sincerity a little false, untruthful?

To begin with, you must do whatever you do of your own free will, with pleasure. The result matters little. You do not foresee it and you are not capable of judging it. But the author has satisfied himself: there is always that.

He has always encumbered himself with unnecessary friendships.

Last night Schwob and I were in despair; there was a moment when I thought we were both about to fly out of the window like bats.

We can no longer be either novelists or journalists. We deserved a certain success, and we had it. Are we simply going to repeat these successes? The praise that used to make us happy now leaves us cold. If someone were to say to us: "Here is money: go away some place for three years and write a masterpiece, which you certainly can write if you wish to," we would not accept. Then what? Are we going to trample on the same spot until we are eighty?

Our talk filled us with a sort of black fever.

Schwob stood up and said he wanted to leave.

He also said that the rarest thing in the world is kindness.

O critic! I understand your criticism very well. Just between us, even I am not always pleased with myself.

Today, when you live in legitimate circumstances, you embarrass everybody. And the men who have mistresses pretend they don't know you.

NOVEMBER

Goncourt complains of the times.

"Nowadays, if you don't want to be forgotten you must produce a masterpiece a year. So I have decided to publish additional parts of my *Journal*—not what concerns me, but what might be of interest. Why don't you come and see me Sunday? I should be very happy."

We separate, and, since we are both going in the same direction, we take opposite sidewalks; and, so that we may not run into each other, I wait until the master, who does not walk fast, gets on ahead. There is marble, today, between the old and the young.

Ollendorf tells me:

"We will reprint *L'Ecornifleur*. When it first appeared, the public was not yet educated."

The brain should always be pure as the air in cold weather.

The language of flowers that speak in *patois*.

Four sinister-looking men were talking about Théophile Gautier as though they had just murdered him.

DECEMBER

At Daudet's. A kindly, almost expansive smile. I observe the faces . . . The men of the hour are Barrès, Schwob, Léon Daudet, and me. Just yesterday, Léon Daudet was saying: "Renard is the most perfect artist I know."

Yesterday, at the Odéon. Marivaux and those sentences of his, pure as crystal, and those pretty love dramas that are like imprisoned torrents.

Whenever I have talked to anyone at too great length, I am like a man who has drunk too much, and, ashamed, doesn't know where to put himself.

It is, when all is said and done, when faced with the subject of death that we feel most bookish.

To leave each thing unfinished, in order to be able to recopy it, later on, with interest and taste.

Roses like bows of white silk.

The way my father's look travels—beginning on the ground, then in small motions reaching my knees, climbing to my chest—the left eye a little behind the right-and finally meeting mine in an union that is embarrassing to both of us. His look is steady only when he is angry, and then his eyeballs stir like two eyeballs inside a nest.

A poet inspired is a poet who writes faulty verse.

The reward of great men is that, long after they have died, one is not quite sure that they are dead.

I don't care about knowing many things: I want to know the things I care about.

1894

[Lautrec] often mentions small men, while seeming to say: "And I'm not so small as all that!" He has a room in a "house," is on good terms with all the ladies, who have feelings of a fineness unknown to honest women, and who pose admirably. He also owns a convent, and he goes from the convent to the "house."

Publication of *Le Vigneron dans sa Vigne*, a small collection of short pieces, and of *Poil de Carotte*, which was to become JR's best-known work. Parts of both had already appeared in periodicals. Poil de Carotte is JR as a child. When, in the *Journal*, he refers to M. or Mme. Lepic he is using fictional names for his own father and mother.

JANUARY

Every moment, life passes on the side of its subject. You have to redo everything it has done, rewrite everything it has created.

As sad to watch as someone you love disappearing into the fog.

To inhale a good whiff of subserviency and respect.

There are no friends; only moments of friendship.

"Well, after all, you too are something of an artist, in your way, since you are a journalist," I am told by M. D., a builder of portable and collapsible houses.

Baïe. The only way she will pull her horse along is by the tail. When it falls, she will not pick it up; she just stamps her feet in anger. No doubt she feels that a horse ought to be able to get to its feet by itself.

The school chum who calls on you because he has seen your name in the paper.

I receive him coolly, but he is full of exuberance. He says:

"Remember the licking I gave you that time?"

To madame:

"If you had seen him! He was biting, howling, foaming with rage!"

To me:

"See? That was how I grabbed you."

He demonstrates on the child. He simulates a struggle.

"Exactly like that! You don't hold it against me? Oh, yes, you're smart in the head, but physically you were never but a puny fellow. Everybody had it in for you. You sure got plenty of lickings!"

The idiot! And he is staying for lunch. I have invited him to lunch! And he will spend the day!

Life can do without logic; literature cannot.

What in the end is most apt to fill me with fever is to leaf through train schedules.

FEBRUARY

He walked noiselessly, like a fish.

When Fantec saw me again after two weeks, he told me I had grown.

I love you as I love that phrase I made up in a dream and which I am unable to remember.

I can say that, thanks to *Poil de Carotte*, I shall have doubled my life.

Thirty years old! Now I am sure that I shall not escape death.

MARCH–Chaumot

The geese had retired, but they could still be heard stirring.

They jabbered, deep in their throats. They raised their wings a little in order to close them more comfortably. They settled down like lathes rustling and thawing together around someone who is about to tell them a piece of gossip.

The cold disorder of Gustave Doré.

To write a book on Chitry, and say, for example: "I knew that pig. I saw him, and I put my cane through the ring of his tail. We are on excellent terms."

I shall love you long enough to see that beauty spot turn into a wart.

The shadow of a dead tree.

Paris

Yesterday, a few of us got together at Vallette's in order to make the *Mercure* into a shareholding company. And we were ashamed of our ignorance, and we tried to conceal it by attempting to look, to nod like businessmen, and we were prudently silent, and when one of us happened to say something, rolling technical terms around his mouth, they sounded painful as mouth-sores.

A peasant is a tree-trunk that walks.

Isn't it possible to dine at people's houses and find them totally without talent?

In order to be truly successful it is necessary, first, that one get there oneself, next, that others do not.

Our life was a lake of friendship through which ran a current of love.

A taste so bad that it is still taste.

Older writers make us angry, but I can see that in two or three years I shall no longer be able to read a book by a young man.

Who will tell, who will paint the strange things I see?

Saw Anatole France yesterday. He talks to me about *L'Écornifleur,* which he likes very, very much. It is always a pleasure to have someone praise you wrongly. I ask him why he called me "the most sincere of naturalists."

"By naturalist," he says, "I mean someone who loves nature." . . .

I say: "My procedure is very simple. I am interested in what I do, and I try to interest others."

And France, with that screwed-on head of his, turns to Veber and says:

"Very good, what he is saying there. It is very good."

To think is to search for clearings in a wood.

"So you believe all those tales?" says Verlaine. "Sir, I get drunk only in order to keep my reputation. I get drunk only when I go out among people."

APRIL

I have a horror of originality.

Happy people have no talent.

All day, I was drugged with sadness.

Man is an animal who lifts his head to the sky and does not see the spiders on his ceiling.

God, he whom everyone knows, by name.

Distrust your fantasy. I only care for cakes that taste a little like bread.

I like rain that lasts all day, and don't feel that I am really in the country until I am well caked with mud.

We spend our lives talking about this mystery: our life.

MAY

All the same, I write nice letters. If people knew, they would want to know me only by correspondence.

My *Journal* must not just be gossip, as the Goncourt's too often is. It must serve to mold my character, ceaselessly to straighten it out.

My soul, which has slid down every declivity, is torn and patched like the seat of a pair of old trousers.

It is not enough to be happy: it is also necessary that others not be.

What is long and difficult is to put oneself into the state of mind, to create the atmosphere, of what one is going to write.

His taste was evident in what he remembered. Selection worked of its own accord in what he had seen. He remembered only the essential.

An episode remembered concerning Léonide Leblanc. When I was presented to her, she remarked:

"True, he is not just an ordinary young man."

And, awkward, my hands on my knees, I suffered the examination of this grande cocotte with badly-shaped ears, who wanted to take me under her wing.

What I write is like letters to myself that I would then permit you to read.

"Why, yes, Fantec, trees are alive."

"But not as alive as me," says he.

Met Mme. Bonnetain yesterday, on the sidewalk. She is just back from the Sudan. Nostrils aquiver, her pretty face to the wind, she was walking arm-in-arm with a little yellow girl dressed in exotic clothes, whom she has adopted and brought back from there. As for the little white girl, the legitimate one, she was walking all by herself in the wake of her mother and her elected sister, who made everyone on the street turn around.

Lifting one's head, one could see up there, between the top branches of the trees, a river of sky flowing.

I did not have what I so much desired, and a while later discovered it was fortunate that I had been denied that stubborn wish.

Who thus protects us?

The thought that I am thirty breaks my heart. A whole dead life behind me. Ahead of me, an opaque stretch in which I see nothing. I feel old, and sad as an old man. My wife looks at me, astonished by my gloom. My Fantec says to me: "So you're getting old, papa?" And, from the outside, no one writes to me; no one sends me a mark of sympathy concerning this lamentable occurrence.

And the trees held the cold moon like an eucharist at the tips of their branches.

JUNE

In his gentle, emphatic voice, Raoul Ponchon said to Mme. S.:

"I had read *L'Ecornifleur*, but I had not imagined Renard as he is. Yes, I like him. I like him because he has qualities I so little expected that I rather thought he had the opposite faults."

Ponchon is a poet who must say: "Women are beautiful, men are gentle, wine is good, and I love life with all of my life."

"Ponchon," says Courteline, "has lived for over twenty-five years in the same house. It has been sold several times, and the different owners always stipulate in the deed that Ponchon will have no rent to pay; all this, without his ever having asked for it."

JULY

Let the hand that writes always ignore the eye that reads!

What does the bird do in a tempest? It does not cling to the branch: it follows the storm.

Do not say that what I write is not true. Everything is true: say that I have written it badly.

A finger of pure water in a crystal thimble.

When I have experienced great difficulty in writing a page, I consider it well written.

OCTOBER

To do for my village what Sainte Beuve did for Chateaubriand and his time . . .

Memory, bring me my countryside, put it here, on the table. The trouble is that before you can remember a place you must see it, and sink your feet into its mud.

He has a style of his own that nobody would want.

To walk around the day your book appears, to cast side glances at the stacks of copies as though you were afraid of the salesman, to hold as a mortal enemy the book merchant who has not put it in the window and who has simply not received it yet, to be like one painfully flayed. Such cakes of soap as books have become! At Flammarion's, I could hear the clerk calling: "One *Poil!* Two *Poil!* Three *Poil!*"

NOVEMBER

[Tristan] Bernard was here this evening, and put me on better terms with myself. He said: "All your friends think that *Poil de Carotte* is the best thing you've done. No one can feel more acutely than I the human quality of your little hero. Toulouse-Lautrec wants to see you . . ."

And here I am, full of glory, blown up with pleasure like a potato, saying: "What a tough métier! Ah! fame is hard to come by, but there's nothing in the world like it."

And I dream of myself surrounded by my friends, giving them advice on will-power and honesty, scattering among them the remarks of a man on his death-bed!

The right word! The right word! What a saving in paper there will be when a law is passed that will force writers to use only the right word!

Lautrec: a tiny blacksmith behind spectacles. A little sack in two compartments to hold his poor legs. Thick lips, and hands as he draws them, with bony, separated fingers, thumbs bent into semicircles. He often mentions small men, while seeming to say: "And I'm not as small as all that!" . . . He has a room in a "house," is on good terms with all the ladies, who have feelings of a fineness unknown to honest women, and who pose admirably. He also owns a convent, and he goes from the convent to the "house."

At first you are pained by his smallness; then he becomes very much alive, very nice, with a sort of grunt that separates his sentences and raises his lips, like the wind puffing out the padded edging of a door . . .

I walk around, I sniff the odors, I listen, a little embarrassed because I do not know the names of all those birds I am disturbing. They are not birds of a thousand colors. These have only one or two; those others, only one.

DECEMBER

The impulse of the pen. Left alone, thought goes as it will. As it follows the pen, it loses its freedom. It wants to go one way, the pen another. It is like a blind man led astray by his cane, and what I come to write is no longer what I wished to write.

Yesterday, in Lautrec's atelier with Tristan Bernard. From a street in which rain was pouring down, we came into a workshop full of stifling heat. In his shirtsleeves, losing his pants, and wearing the hat of a flour merchant, the little Lautrec opened the door. First of all, I see, on a sofa in the rear, two naked women: one shows her belly, the other her backside. Bernard goes up to them to shake hands, saying: "Good-day, young ladies!" I, in a state of embarrassment, haven't the courage to look squarely at the two models. I look around for a place to put my hat, my coat, my dribbling umbrella.

"Don't let us keep you from working," says Bernard.

"We are through," says Lautrec. "Get yourselves dressed, ladies."

And he fetches a ten-franc piece and places it on the table. They get dressed, partly behind canvasses, and, from time to time, I risk a glance, without succeeding in seeing anything properly; I seem to feel their defiant looks cast upon my blinking eyes. At last, they go. I have seen dull-skinned buttocks, pendulous breasts, red hair, yellow fur.

Lautrec shows us studies he has made in "houses," the work of his youth: it was from the beginning bold and ugly. He strikes me as being especially curious about art. I am not sure that what he is doing is good, but I know that he likes what is rare, and that he is an artist. This little man who calls his cane "my little stick," who certainly suffers because of his size, deserves, because of his sensitivity, to be a man of talent.

I was born for successes in journalism, for the daily renown, the literature of abundance: reading great writers changed all that. That was the misfortune of my life.

Alphonse Daudet tells me:

"In spite of my admiration for *Poil de Carotte*, I still prefer your short pieces in *Le Vigneron dans sa Vigne*. I know nothing more perfect in French literature. You make thumbnail masterpieces.

"You are a man of the seventeenth century. You should have a stipend from a king or a nobleman, because we shall never be able to pay for what you do, which is so special, so much your own, that I don't believe you could do anything else . . . You are now in full limelight. All your admirers, and I the first among them, will knock themselves out to get you whatever you want, and I mean what I say . . . Ask for something, the moon if you want it, and we shall get it for you."

Since then, I wake up every morning with the bliss of not having to go to an office.

Suppose, instead of earning a lot of money in order to live, we should try to live on little money?

1895

I desire nothing from the past. I do not count on the future.
The present is enough for me. I am a happy man,
for I have renounced happiness.

JR leases a former presbytery in Chaumot, close to Chitry. His life will henceforth be
divided between this place and Paris.

JANUARY

The good that one expects does not come to pass, but unexpected
good does. There is justice, but he who dispenses it is playful. He is
a jovial judge, who laughs at us, plays tricks on us, but who, when
all is weighed, never makes a mistake.

Visit to the zoo:
   Tiny parakeets, like tie-pins that sing.

FEBRUARY

How monotonous snow would be if God had not created crows!

Last night, we cast around for a name for our house in Chaumot. Fixed upon "La Gloriette," because this means a small summer house, and also because it is a diminutive of *gloire*, which puts an obligation on a man of letters.

L'Herbe—I want to try to put a village into a book, to put it in entire, from the mayor to the pig. And those who will understand the beauty of the title will be the ones who have heard the peasant say: "The grass is growing," or "It's good weather for grass," or "There is no grass left."

I acquired this house to find happiness. Papon, when I met him, said: "Well, *you* look happy!"

And I replied: "My good Papon, I don't just look happy, I am."

"That's because you've been lucky," he said. "Things have worked out right for you."

And he walked on. What if he should be right! What if I should just have been lucky, I who imagine that I created my happiness out of my hard work, my perseverance, my sense of life, let's come out with it: my brains! What if it was just luck!

There are a few essential needs, and one should depart from them neither inwardly nor outwardly. Outwardly, it is foolishness; inwardly, it is pride.

From my window, I see the canal, the river, woods. I shall disdain nothing, and if I could in conscience go into politics, I would do so.

As a child, I had the reputation of being a hot-head. Now, in my own beloved country, I shall have to build myself a reputation for kindness.

The light, winged heat of a wood fire.

There are good writers and great ones. Let us be the good ones.

Yes, the story I am writing exists, written in absolutely perfect fashion, some place, in the air. All I must do is find it, and copy it.

You can recover from the writing malady only by falling mortally ill and dying.

Thank God, Achilles and Don Quixote are well enough known so that we can dispense with reading Homer and Cervantes.

In literature, the real is distinguishable from the false as fresh flowers are from artificial flowers: by a sort of inimitable scent.

Toulouse-Lautrec. The oftener you see him, the taller he grows. He ends up by being taller than average.

What a delightful quip! It should be used some place. He says so many delightful things that he no longer knows where to put them.

MARCH

Last night, banquet for Edmond de Goncourt. You may, if you wish, send a telegram excusing yourself, thereby saving 12 francs. And then, the telegram is read over the dessert, and you have called attention to yourself . . .

"We don't see you often," Goncourt tells me.

"Mon cher Maître, I stay away purely out of discretion."

"Well, it's silly."

"There is a word I like."

He is handsome, our old master. He is moved, and when you shake his hand, it feels soft and wavering, as though filled with the water of his emotion.

On the table in front of him, a magnificent cake, something like a pastry-cook's model of the Académie Goncourt.

What! is that the great Clemenceau, that gentleman talking with one hand in his pocket, in an abrupt voice and old-fashioned phraseology? . . . Goodness, how far those people are removed from us! "Good workingman . . . social Republic . . ." Come, come, sir, you are among men of letters, and you are mistaking us for voters. Don't you sense our disappointment, even to a certain extent our scorn? . . .

And at last, Daudet, remaining seated, reads to Goncourt his little exercise in friendship. He really looks like a schoolboy at his table, bent over his tremulous sheet of paper, under the stern eye of the master. And yet I declare that all our sympathy went out to them when, in the midst of our bravos and applause, Goncourt and Daudet pressed each other's hands under the table . . .

Georges Hugo, bunting with all the health of one of his grandfather's alexandrines . . .

And I felt like going immediately to no matter what school ceremony, to make my first speech. My voice lifted; my gestures formed of their own accord.

Yes! Tonight I am happy because a few men of taste have expressed admiration for me. But tomorrow?

Claudel reads us his literal translation of Aeschylus's *Agamemnon*. After demurring modestly, he begins, with his voice that sounds like a talking machine, and his lips that open like heat lightning. His head is of an ashen shade. . . . He admires or detests playfully. He says:

"There is nothing more beautiful than the Chinese theatre. Once you have seen that, you wish to see nothing more."

Then he reads us a revision of *Tête d'Or*, which he will be rewriting all his life.

"You are right," I say. "We should all, in the spring of each year, spend a month correcting our past work."

We talked for over five hours, and nothing of it has remained with me. We scorned, in turn, money, and work that brought in none. I said: "I love solitude," and Claudel said: "You don't know what solitude is. I have known it in an American desert, some eighty kilometers from Boston, where my violinist friend composed an air that contained the desert entire."

The little premonitory shiver that comes when a beautiful sentence is about to take shape.

Schwob knows which is the weakest part in a book, and that the author must be complimented on that part particularly.

With its purring, the cat accompanies the tick-tock of the clock; it is the only music in the room.

[Goncourt] so affected, the night of his banquet, that he kept for himself the entire basket of flowers sent by Mme. Mirbeau containing little nosegays for guests of distinction.

APRIL

To Charles Maurras: "As a writer, I try to set limits for myself. As a reader, I set no limits. Believe me, I am fond of a great many things you would not guess, from my books. I have been deeply stirred by the poets, and especially the prodigious verbal abundance of Victor Hugo. Am I reacting against this? It is possible. But I am, rather, practicing delimitation. Beyond those limits I feel ill at ease, and I seek an excuse by persuading myself that, in order to do well, I must do little, and even work on a small scale. But when I raise my head from that desk where you think I am contracting myself, I can assure you that I scorn no one, and I am not afraid of admiring the greatest writers. It is even a pleasant relaxation to let myself go."

I desire nothing from the past. I do not count on the future. The present is enough for me. I am a happy man, for I have renounced happiness.

In this Oscar Wilde affair, if there is something more comical than the indignation of all England, it is the show of being shocked on the part of certain Frenchmen with whom we are well acquainted.

Rostand, youngish, oldish, baldish, full of an attractive talent in his *Princesse Lointaine*, and thoroughly conversant with *L'Ecornifleur* and *Cocquecigrues*.

MAY

Mallarmé. His conversation is so clear that, after one has read him, his talk seems banal. He talks of Baudelaire, of what I am doing. In spite of myself I remain icy. I can't manage to say a pleasant word. If, at least, he were hairy like a wild beast, I could stroke him.

What pleases women most is gross flattery concerning their intelligence.

JUNE

[In Belgium] It is not a joke, or a mirage: a beautiful young girl is walking barefoot on the road.

A lightweight moon, as though made out of a piece of white cloud.

Claudel. The stern country of the Vosges, where he was born a second time. His brow must have bumped against the sides of the mountains, and his gaze gone speeding down valleys that extend beyond sight. A cross planted on a hill where the height makes you reel. A church that smothers a village in its shadow, and those pious people who, always, always, look at you as one looks at strangers.

JULY

All our criticism consists of reproaching others with not having the qualities that we believe ourselves to have.

AUGUST

Tristan Bernard, a bold man, a real Parisian. He has the courage of getting off his bicycle and buying a sack of grapes from the fruit vendor across the street; and then to eat them at once, on the sidewalk, under the eyes of the concierges of the neighborhood.

I am often dissatisfied with what I have written. I am never dissatisfied with what I am writing, because if I were, I would not be writing it.

SEPTEMBER

My brain is stuffed with literature, and swollen like a goose's liver.

At every moment Poil de Carotte returns to me. We live together, and I only hope that I die before he does.

Histoires naturelles. Buffon described animals to please men. I should like to please the animals themselves. I wish, if they could read my little *Histoires naturelles*, that they would smile.

I want my ear to be a shell that keeps in itself all the sounds of nature.

Be modest! It is the kind of pride least likely to offend.

OCTOBER

He who loves literature does not love money, or paintings, or bibelots, or all the rest. At bottom, Balzac did not care about literature.
Balzac is true in the overall picture, not in the details.

At work in the morning: at first, mist, sometimes impenetrable. And, gradually, clearing. It is like a small sun slowly rising in the brain.

Allais tells me: "I have just met Hervieu [Paul Hervieu, playwright], who says to me: 'Have you ever heard of such ill luck? The Théâtre Français has closed for tonight because of the death of Pasteur!' And he has a fixed income of 15,000 francs!"

Chaumot

My brother Maurice tells me: "Papa and I sit together on the wall. He waits for me to talk, and I wait for him. And that goes on until we go to bed." He can no longer shoot. He has a pain in the left arm. When a partridge starts out from somewhere, or a hare goes barreling off, he can't lift his arm. It is as though someone were to put a hand on his shoulder to prevent him from killing, saying: "That's enough!"

In the old bedroom, the paper is coming off the walls and the plaster is crumbling. Holes are forming. There is one big enough for me to put my watch into, as in a niche.

Papa walked with me as far as the Bargeot fields, and he wearies me. When we got back, he said: "I am no more tired than when we started, because at my age you are always tired."

Papa as mayor.

The town drummer receives 25 francs a year.

"It is not enough to keep his drum in condition," I say.

"In the first place, the drum does not belong to him. The only drumming he does is at election time. Supposing I keep him busy one hour a year, that is an hour well paid. Besides, it is a privilege . . .

"Every community now has free medical assistance; and we give bread to the poor. There are poor in Chitry, but not one beggar. With a piece of bread and a few nuts, you can live. Beggars are not permitted to leave their community. There were two that came to me from Saint-Révérien, a blind man led by a young woman. I told him:

"'But couldn't your wife work instead of walking around like that all day long?'

"'Well, monsieur le maire, that would bring in less.'

"I gave them a sou anyway, telling them never to come back, or I should have them arrested. Then I watched them go away over the old road. I could hear them laughing. They were making fun of me."

Nature is not definitive. One can always add to it.

Jules Renard, Mayor of Chaumot—now, that will look well on the covers of my books!

NOVEMBER

Papa. The swollen veins of his temples. Moles are digging around and ravaging him under the skin.

Rostand really has a nicety beyond everything. He does not do any journalism, does not write for reviews, for fear of taking someone's job. But, since he doesn't have those daily successes to whip him on, he sometimes remains in a state of despair two or three months on end. He is very much preoccupied with the misery of the world, and gives much to charity.

The truly free man is the one who will turn down an invitation to dinner without giving an excuse.

Be interesting! Be interesting! Art is no excuse for boring people.

Literature, a queer sort of occupation: the less one produces, the better it must be.

DECEMBER

Modesty is becoming to the great. What is difficult is to be modest when one is a nobody.

Funeral of the father of Courteline [satiric writer]. Courteline's eyes were full of tears. The sorrow of an intelligent man is more painful to see than that of a fool.

I don't mind signing the petition for Oscar Wilde, with the proviso that he will give his word of honor to stop—writing.

I have put too much of my life into my work. I am no longer anything but a gnawed bone.

Descaves wants to persuade me that I shall need fifty *Histoires naturelles* to make a volume. It isn't his opinion alone: others share it. Lautrec suggests that he illustrate eight of them and that we sell a hundred copies at twenty-five francs a piece. We would share the profit.

Sarah Bernhardt. I try to find a phrase that will sum up my impressions. I find only this: "She is nice." I had not wished to see her. Now I have destroyed the ridiculous and awkward idol I had made of her. What remains is a woman whom I had believed thin and who is plump, whom I had believed ugly and who is pretty, yes, pretty as a child's smile. When Rostand said: "May I present Jules Renard," she rose at once from her [dressing] table and said in a tone that was joyous, childlike, adorable:

"Oh, how glad I am! He is just as I thought he was, isn't he, Rostand? Monsieur, I am an admirer of yours."

"Madame, it is the amazement of my life to learn that you can admire the works (I said: *The Works*) of Jules Renard."

"Why?" she said. "Did you think I was a fool?"

"There! I said something stupid."

"Not at all!"

And she puts on lip rouge.

Later on, on the stairs, I found this to say: "No, madame, I took you for a woman of genius, with all the inconveniences that entails." Which was probably even more stupid.

"Feel how cold I am?" she says, brushing Rostand's cheek with her hand. She calls him "her poet," "her author."

"That's true. It is frozen," says Rostand.

And I can find no words! Not a chance of being brilliant. I am very strongly affected, taken, and I should like to be a man of the world.

"What are you doing now, Renard?"

"Madame, I have just done something beautiful: I have been listening to you."

"Yes, you are a love. But what are you doing?"

"Oh, nothing much. Little nothings, natural histories about animals. They are less handsome than this one," I say, indicating her dog, a magnificent dog she calls Djemm, I believe.

And my poor man's voice is lost in the dog's fur.

"Do you know whom you resemble?" she says. "Have you been told?"

"Yes: Rochefort."

"No: Albert Delpit."

Two other voices:

"Duflos" . . . "Lemaître."

It strikes me that I resemble far too many people.

"And you liked Albert Delpit, madame?"

"No."

"Oh!"

"But I like you. Delpit turned out badly. You will turn out well. Besides, it's too late now. You can no longer go off in a wrong direction."

Around us, there is evidence of some surprise that the tragedienne is paying so much attention to me. "Who is it?" they ask. Some know, others do not.

Then she goes off alone to play the most beautiful tragedy in the world.

Why does she add "e"s to words where there are none? I'll have to get used to that. I have got used to it. Already, my heart is full of gratitude toward her, of the desire to admire, to love, and the fear of letting myself go. I spin out dry little theories to Rostand on the wariness I had felt toward her, and the pleasure I now feel over having found her nice, yes, nice.

1896

Sarah Bernhardt. When she comes down the winding staircase of the hotel, it looks as though she were standing still, while the staircase turns around her.

Publication of *Histoires naturelles*, a small collection of animal sketches, and of *La Maîtresse*, a novel. Encouraged by Lucien Guitry, JR works on a one-act play, *Le Plaisir de Rompre*.

JANUARY

Chez Sarah Bernhardt. Near a monumental fireplace, she reclines on the pelt of a polar bear. Because in her house you do not sit down, you recline. She says to me: "Put yourself here, Monsieur Renard." Here? Where? Between her and Mme. Rostand there is a cushion. Not daring to sit upon it, I kneel at Mme. Rostand's feet, and mine stretch way, way out, as in a confessional.

They fear the number thirteen. Maurice Bernhardt is there, with his pregnant young wife. Sarah takes my arm to go into the dining room. It is enough to make me forget to lift the portière. I let her go as soon as we get to the first plate, but it is way over there that we must go, to that big chair with a canopy. I sit at her right, and do not expect to eat much. Sarah drinks out of a golden cup. I cannot bring myself to open my mouth, not even to ask for my napkin, which a footman has carried away; and I eat my meat with the fruit fork. A moment later I catch myself neatly placing my sucked asparagus stems across my knife holder. I am also stopped by a certain platter made out of glass: it is for the salad. Fortunately, there is on Sarah's left one of those inevitable doctors that one finds in novels, on the stage, and in real life. He explains to Sarah why it is that last night she heard twenty-one knocks, and why her dog barked twenty-one times.

Then, palms are scrutinized. I am under the influence of the moon. I must love the moon, speak of it, be influenced by its variations. It is true that I talk a great deal about the moon, but I seldom look at it. In my thumb there is more will-power than logic. That is true. Rostand is the opposite; and Sarah takes and retakes my hand, which is white and plump, but with ill-kept fingernails. I have never seen them as they are tonight, neither handsome nor too clean.

"Oh, we have made a study of that!" says Maurice Bernhardt from the end of the table.

I am rather inclined to believe that Sarah makes it up. Besides, she finds nothing.

Then Mme. Maurice Bernhardt spills over the tablecloth a glass containing water and flowers. I am soaked. Quickly, Sarah dips her fingers in the water and rubs my head. That will keep me happy a long time.

Her rule is never to think of the morrow. Tomorrow may be anything, even death. She makes something of every minute . . . And I tell her what I thought about her at the time of my first visit:

"You are plump, pretty and nice."

The Sarah I know through her fame, who covers a half-century, disturbs me and makes me dizzy; but the woman I have here, near me, does not impress me too much.

And then we have jokes: "Do you know why frogs have no tails? . . . Neither do I." And so on. It is hard to remember you are in the house of someone "great." Then there are the resemblances with animals. Sarah is sure she looks like an antelope, Rostand like a rodent, his wife like a sheep, Maurice like a greyhound, his wife like an owl. As for me, one doesn't know. I may have too much brow for an animal.

"I had hardly read a line of yours," says Sarah, "when I thought: that man must have red hair. But redheads are ill-natured. Besides, you are rather on the blond side."

And more nonsense of this sort.

Haraucourt gravely proclaims my admiration for Victor Hugo. "He was so witty!" says Sarah. Hugo gave her a ring, the "tear" of Ruy Blas.

In the salon. Potted palms with an electric bulb under each leaf. Under a glass bell, a little girl made of brown clay, which Sarah will finish when she comes back. Portraits, and a lot of museum objects.

Less of an actress than most, she says:

"I've wanted to do everything–write, sculpt. Oh, I know I have no talent whatsoever, but I wanted to try everything."

In comes the lion, one of the five pumas of Sarah Bernhardt. He is led in on a chain. He goes around sniffing at skins and people. He has a terrible extension of the hindquarters, claws, and Haraucourt does well to close his eyes when the puma shows an inclination to caress his shirt front. At last, more or less to everyone's relief, he is led away.

Next come two enormous dogs with pink pug noses: each of them might eat a child for his supper. They roll on the floor, gentle, well-behaved, and pretty soon our clothes are covered with little white hairs.

A bottle of champagne turns over in the footman's hands. The cork goes off, and Sarah, stretched out on her bearskin, receives the bath full in the face. For a minute, I thought it was part of the entertainment.

The funeral of Verlaine. As a certain academician said, funerals excite me. They return me to vitality. Lepelletier had his mouth full of tears. He cried out that women had ruined Verlaine: that at least is ingratitude toward Verlaine. Moréas said: "Of course."

Barrès has just the right kind of voice for speaking over a grave, with sonorities that bring to mind vaults and crows. Indeed, he spoke admirably of the younger generation, while Beaubourg felt that he was rather pulling the covers to his side, because it is really Anatole France who made Verlaine. Before beginning to speak, he handed his hat to Montesquiou. I had an impulse to applaud by tapping my cane against the tomb, but what if the dead man had wakened?

Mendès spoke of stairs of pale marble on which, between oleanders, one would ascend toward radiant candles. It was very pretty, and could be applied to anyone.

Coppée was applauded at first. A coolness followed when he reserved his place in Heaven next to Verlaine. Begging his pardon . . .

Mallarmé. I shall have to read his speech again. Lepelletier made a materialistic profession of faith, although there were no electors around.

The great quality of Barrès is tact. He would say the right thing with his mouth full.

Donnay introduced himself to me: the first time I have found Verlaine useful.

Verlaine had gone to Holland to lecture. The best room had been reserved for him. He summoned the manager:

"I want another room."

"Maître, this is our best one."

"Precisely! That is what I say: I want another one."

He had brought a suitcase, which contained only a dictionary.

Vicaire seems to be taking over the succession of Verlaine on his very grave. He was already quite drunk, and Spont had almost to lift him into a hackney-cab.

At the restaurant, jokes. A table is reserved and a repast ordered for the funeral of Coppée.

How much finer we should be if we were not afraid of being duped!

I love Rostand, and I am happy to make others, Bernard, Boulanger, love him. He is my "*prince lointain*," a little brother whose suffering face pains me. I am constantly afraid of learning of his death, of having him glide out of my arms. He is delicate and nice, and without meanness. He may be very unhappy. He avoids faces he does not know, and is happy to know that he is loved. Yes, it may be that, with all his luxury, his pretty wife, his nascent fame, he is very unhappy. His death would cause me very, very much grief.

To take notes is to play the scales of literature.

FEBRUARY

Mallarmé. His verses are to a certain extent music, yes, as free verse is to a certain extent drawing.

"Lautrec is so small," says Mme. T. Bernard, "that it makes my head spin to look at him."

"I applauded you very much, the other night, in *Amants*."
"And I," says Guitry, "admire you always. You ought to give us something for the stage." . . .
"That is an encouragement."
"Take it as an engagement."
"I'll see you again in a month."
And here I am, full of fever, before my eyes a theatre blazing with my success. What good, what wonderful times I am about to have!

Rostand. He has a beautiful study: he does not work there. He works in a bedroom, on a rickety little table . . .

He isolates himself more and more. He finds us insincere, untruthful, spiteful, and greedy.

I have only one reason left for being fond of Rostand: the fear that he may soon die.

"Well? what do you want to say to me?"

That is how he greets me, after having let me cool my heels.

"You are insufferable!" I tell him. "I shall remain young, and leave you to that old age you have chosen. Good-day!"

"Let's break off!"

His eyes are small and narrow. He curls his mustache. He is pale . . . As I am closing the door, I hear:

"What a filthy nuisance!"

I turn around. I say *au revoir*, and that the air is lovely.

"Amuse yourself," he says.

I am shaking, and his lips are white. And perhaps we are both experiencing a savage joy to be turning our backs upon each other.

One friend less, what a relief!

Rostand. I wish him a good illness, which would bring him to the threshold of death and then make him retrace his way toward life.

The reconciliation of two friends. Suddenly, the heart, which was dry, hard and shrivelled, softens and expands, as though it had fallen into pure water.

A pomegranate that laughs like a Negro.

I have neither memory nor intelligence, and I am an artist only as a result of a lot of training, hut I receive certain impressions with such intensity that in this I can measure up to the greatest men.

The mimosa is among flowers what the canary is among birds.

MARCH

Guitry. Yesterday, in his dressing room, I watched him messing around like a big, hairy actress. Little pots of cream and rouge. His watch is in front of him.

"Monsieur Guitry, they're only waiting for you."

"Let them wait! they can't start without me." . . .

He has put into fashion necks with a goiter in the back.

The little light existing in the mystery that surrounds us comes from ourselves: it is a false light. The mystery has never shown us its own.

APRIL

When he drinks with a couple, he always pays, so that people may believe he is the lover.

In the desert, she would ask for a chair so she could sit down.

Marc Stéphane, the author of *Fleurs de Morphine*, sends me his girl friend to ask if I do not intend to write a piece on his book in the *Echo de Paris* or the *Mercure de France*. She wears her hair in flat bands under a little yellow hat, has yellow teeth and full cheeks, and a heavy accent. She is at the same time brazen and innocent.

And I play the master . . . And I am flattered. Just imagine! It is the first time that a woman has called on me. She doesn't unhook her bodice, but that, too, will come. Long live French literature! The profession has its good side. All the same, it bothers me to do that piece . . .

After the Corneilles, the Racines, the great dreamers, came the La Bruyères, the La Rochefoucaulds, the great men of reality.

I tell you, cher Maître, with Hugo, Lamartine, Chateaubriand, genius climbed too high. It broke its back. Now it drags along the road like a village goose.

MAY–Chaumot

Don't imagine that there are unknown great men.

By six o'clock in the morning, she has finished cleaning her house. Someone may go by her door, who stops and talks. This talk may go on till noon, and the rest of the day is spent in the same way.

No one ever sees her working. You knock. She opens the door, in wooden shoes, neat and clean, her hands over her belly. Everything is in order. How does she keep busy? Sometimes, she knits. She is so happy over having lost her husband who drank, and beat her, that even the death of one of her two boys did not sadden her. She could go on living like this for ever.

Life is short, but how long it is between life and death!

When I returned to the country, the morning greeted me with the song of larks sparkling in the air like flames at the ends of tall candles.

At night the dead trees stretch out their delicate skeletons.

And those long-drawn-out days in which one could write an entire book.

JUNE

There is in me a substratum of coarseness that allows me to understand peasants and to enter deeply into their lives.

The wind passes its invisible hand through the leaves.

An old peasant naked: what a sight!

I feel as sad as a country Verlaine.

At the beginning of winter, it is a custom here for the rural guard to go around with a mason and make a security inspection of all the houses in the village. They examine the chimney, hand-test the oven, and have a drop to drink. At the tenth house, they are tipsy. Each receives three francs a day, and the job lasts three days.

This year, when Papon came to tell the mayor that he was to start his rounds, my father, who had already had to sack him last year, did away with this custom, which rests on no legal base.

"If it pays you nine francs, I'd rather pay you eighteen to keep you in order."

In spite of the liquor, Papon answered: "As you wish. It makes no difference to me, monsieur le maire."

But papa forgot to give him the eighteen francs.

She is original enough to be of the opinion that the lily is a stupid flower.

JULY

Ragotte. [The wife of Philippe; a village couple. They work for the Renards.] She walks through life. She goes toward death with her wheelbarrow full of wash.

It is cheating to try to be kind. You must be born kind or never meddle with it.

I should like to cause living literature, life in literature, to take a small step forward.

I am made only to listen to the earth and watch it live.

Philippe and his wife responsive to the song of birds at two o'clock in the morning.

Put a little moon into what you write.

I should like to have been one of those great men who had few things to say and said them in few words.

A cat that has not become used to her tail. When suddenly she catches sight of it, she pounces upon it and wheels upon herself like a drunken sun.

Death of Goncourt. Regret at not having been to see him more often: twice in my lifetime.

Incapable of sustained effort, I read here and there, and write here and there. But I do believe that this is the lot of the true artist.

When I notice something ridiculous, I notice it only much later. I do not observe a moment while I am living it. It is only later that I go over every detail of my life.

As though he had read Fénelon on *L'Education des Filles*, papa was always setting Jesus Christ before us as an example: "Until he was thirty, Jesus Christ worked in a shop." Perfectly true, but it became tiresome after a while.

AUGUST

Every day, write your page: but if you feel it is bad, stop. Never mind! It will be a day lost, but it is better to do nothing than to do it badly.

Verlaine. It is very simple: He had the genius of a god and the heart of a pig. Those who lived close to him must have suffered. It was their own fault—they made the mistake of being there.

Let us always keep, even in the midst of our greatest joys, a corner of sadness at the bottom of our soul; to serve as refuge in case of sudden alarm.

OCTOBER

"Oh, God!" cried Mme. Lepic. "What have I done to be so miserable! Oh, my poor Poil de Carotte, if I ever tormented you, please forgive me!"

She wept like the gutter on the roof.

Then suddenly, her face dry:

"If my poor leg did not give me so much pain I would run away from here. I would earn my living washing dishes in a rich house."

There is nothing harder to look at than the face of a mother you do not love and for whom you are sorry.

The secret Poil de Carotte.

I wish I were a great writer so that I could tell it in words so exact that they would not seem too natural.

Mme. Lepic was given to changing her chemise in front of me. In order to tie up the laces over her woman's breast, she would lift her arms and her neck. Again, as she warmed herself by the fire, she would tuck her dress up above her knees. I would be compelled to see her thigh; yawning, or with her head in her hands, she would rock on her chair. My mother, of whom I cannot speak without terror, used to set me on fire.

That fire has remained in my veins. In the daytime it sleeps, but at night it wakens, and I have frightful dreams. In the presence of M. Lepic, who is reading his paper and doesn't even look our way, I take possession of my mother, who is offering herself to me, and I re-enter that womb from whence I came. My head disappears into her mouth. The pleasure is infernal. What a painful awakening there will be tomorrow, and how dejected I shall be all day! Immediately afterward we are enemies again. Now I am the stronger. With those same arms that were passionately embracing her, I throw her to the ground, I crush her; I stamp on her, I grind her face against the tiles of the kitchen floor.

My father, inattentive, continues to read his paper.

If I knew that tonight I should again have that dream, I swear I would flee from the house instead of going to bed and to sleep. I would walk until dawn, and I would not drop from exhaustion, because fear would keep me on my feet, sweating and on the run.

The ridiculous added to the tragic: my wife and children call me Poil de Carotte.

When we are about to leave, maman gives a box to Marinette. It contains a chicken, butter, fruit, and she says:

"Be sure to send the box back! Take good care of it!" And she sings the praises of her box.

She knows perfectly well that Marinette will return it to her filled with coffee and good things from Paris.

NOVEMBER

Sometimes Baïe addresses me with such gravity that I find myself replying in the tone of an upper-class footman.

It is at the cost of all my anguish that I give to others an impression of perfect security.

When I left Mme. Sarah Bernhardt I was in a mood to write a fine epic poem, if I had the time.

DECEMBER

Sarah Bernhardt. When she comes down the winding staircase of the hotel, it looks as though she were standing still, while the staircase turns around her.

I do not know how to help a woman into a wrap. I place Mme. Rostand's on her shoulders inside out, and I don't hand her the shoe horn properly. I tell her:

"Some day, when we're alone in a corner, you will have to let me kiss your hand so I can find out what it's all about."

"It is just a little above the wrist," she says, "that it begins to take on taste."

Sarah rises. The same adorable business on the stairs. At the top, Jules Chancel awaits her and catches her hand as she passes.

Sarah is, if one may call it that, an extraordinary "heart-catcher." She may not have talent, but after her day, which is the day of all of us, in which we love one another, are devoted to one another, we feel renewed, grown taller; and this state of over-stimulation is a blessing, and if, the next day, we are without talent, we are nothing but fools.

[Sarah recites on the stage a sonnet by Edmond Rostand]. Incredible success for Rostand, who says, with perfect aplomb, Thanks to the eyes of Sarah Bernhardt. A success as though his sonnet were in five acts, and the applause for Rostand is one with the applause for Sarah. It does not seem to end, and it is unforgettable. She is the only one to uphold the throne, and we are all her faithful subjects, prostrate at her feet. . . .

[Sarah Bernhardt to JR] "You think I'm silly, don't you?"

"I think you're marvelous."

"I want to be silly today. Do you want to kiss me?"

I do believe that she has to say it twice. She kisses me, simply, on both cheeks. I kiss her just a little on a corner of her mouth, not daring to press. And I say to the Rostands, to the others:

"Am I happy! Sarah Bernhardt kissed me! I kissed Sarah Bernhardt!" . . .

Yes, yes, let it be admitted: Sarah is Genius.

She sets me upright, like a bolt of lightning . . .

In the crowd waiting for you at the door, there are rich men whose worth lies only in admiring you; and beggars who stand up like the great of the earth because they are about to see Sarah go by. . . . O Sarah, you are Genius!

And, every evening, there is a happy man who is seeing Sarah for the first time.

We did not have the same thoughts, but we had thoughts of the same color.

The feet of birds make little lilac sprigs on the snow.

At a sign of Sarah Bernhardt I would follow her to the ends of the earth, with my wife.

A morning so gray that the birds went back to bed.

There is no paradise on earth, but there are pieces of it. What there is on earth is a broken paradise.

Signs of winter . . . The rooster on the steeple looks obstinately north. The weather is too bad to pull up the potatoes. All this mud— it's too much. Let us go away! The chimneys smoke. Already, that hollow sound of the doors that makes the heart sick. Villages, that a few leaves were enough to hide, appear quite bare. A falling leaf uncovers the horizon.

Painters can always say that their picture is badly lighted.

We are never happier than when our jokes have made the maid laugh.

It is in the cafés of small towns that one sees humanity at its most hideous.

To rub one's hands like a fly.

The real sky is the one you see at the bottom of the water.

1897

"I have a hundred clippings," I say, "testifying to the success of Plaisir de Rompre.*" Why do I say a hundred, when I know quite well there are not over seventy?*

JANUARY

I have not renounced ambition. The fire still burns in me—a banked fire, but alive.

A man in love with truth need not be either great or a poet. He is both without trying.

"I have just seen a shooting star," says Philippe. "It fell at the bottom of the garden."

There is jealousy in admiration as there is in love. If you do not believe that I am the one who admires you most, I admire you no longer.

What a sad sight—an old woman in a fine carriage with two horses!

I am like a house that, not being able to change its place, would open its windows in order to fill itself with the unknown; but nothing enters, and meanwhile the house has lost its intimacy.

I shall anticipate you. I tell you my intimate life, as I see it, all true. Thus, you will not have to make up a false one after my death. Otherwise, you would have to do a little repair job, like the biographers of Mérimée.

When I think of the letters I write, I wonder what value, from the standpoint of sincerity, one is justified in giving to the correspondence of great men.

Valéry, a prodigious conversationalist. From the Café de la Paix to the *Mercure de France*, he displayed amazing riches of mind, a real fortune. He brings everything down to mathematics. He would like to make a table of logarithms for writers. This is why Mallarmé interests him so much. He tries to find in him a syntax of precision. He would like to do for each sentence what has already been done for words: show its genesis. He has a contempt for intelligence. He says that strength has the right to arrest intelligence and clap it in jail. Too much intelligence brings on an aversion for itself.

You will not have made real progress until you have lost the desire to prove your talent.

"The people" must not be confused with "the peasant." I am closer to the peasant, and I don't mean that I take pride in it. Sometimes I profit by it, and sometimes I suffer from it.

De Flers has just gone out of here, after telling me that [Jeanne] Granier will play *Le Plaisir de Rompre*, that she already knows it by heart, that she is trying out the lines. And Noblet, who likes everything I've done, will probably take the part of the man. So all this month I'm going to feel foolish and miserable. I exclaim: "What luck!" and I don't know what I have done to deserve it.

My work, played by Granier, who, says de Flers, does not ask to be paid! My work, played by Noblet, who, says de Flers, will act without a fee! I am lost! If, at least, I had planned it! Ah! How lucky I am!

"Listen," says Marinette. "You deserve it. You have such very tough moments to go through."

FEBRUARY

Granier. *Le Plaisir de Rompre.* . . . "The minute I read your play, I thought; 'That man will have to write a three-act play for me. He's the man for me.'"

As soon as she opens her mouth, I tell her:

"How intelligent you are! I am enchanted with your intelligence, your charm."

After I have left, she will say: "He's comical, that guy!"

Lautrec is waiting for the death of old Victoria. As soon as the news comes, he will make off for London to see a spectacle unique in this century. Allais says that she sustains herself only by drinking gin.

Yesterday, first rehearsal. The reading begins with Granier and Mayer [no explanation is given as to why Noblet was replaced by Henry Mayer] separated by a table, bottles, cups of coffee and smells of cheese.

She understands quickly and sets the tone. Mayer is slower and surer. Granier suggests a good change in the handling of the letter. She can't bring herself to say: "I was already thinking." I thanked her. Soon there will be nothing of my own left. With a charming selfishness, she tells me she expects to act the play here, there, and everywhere, and that I must not have it published.

We separate enchanted with one another. Everybody is doing well.

Pretty soon, we shall have to announce a play by Jeanne Granier and Jules Renard. She might not discover anything for others, but she is intelligent for what is suitable for herself. Her roguish face attracts words that tell. It is a special sort of intelligence, but it is intelligence, which induces me to feel modest.

At a certain passage, she says:

"I'd like to laugh here!"

She looks for her intonations inside of her, and her face takes on an "elsewhere" look; then suddenly the sentence jumps out, with the right emphasis.

"Victor Hugo wrote *Ruy Blas* in nineteen days," said Bernard.

"Yes, but he would not have written one chapter of the *Caractères* [La Bruyère]. It is the difference between something beautiful, even sublime, and something perfect. The perfect is always a little mediocre."

MARCH

It is beyond all my dreams. Granier, ah! what a dress and what a setting! She has brought statuettes, sheet-music, flowers, a lamp, and a lampshade that she made, herself, that very morning. And is she pretty! It is the first time that she moves me. I don't dare kiss her. With his first lines, Mayer makes people laugh. From that moment on, I am swimming in bliss, too much so. Everything carries. I walk around in the back.

The theatre is packed. Everywhere people standing.

At the end, Granier has tears of silver in her voice.

I hear: "Ah! Ah! Bravo!" I think I'm on the moon, and it seems like a joke, a most pleasant one.

Three curtain calls. Photograph. It is, I think, as great a success as can be obtained from so small a thing. And no false note. Then, the filing past. Hands, hands, hands . . . Descaves, who has led the applause, looks happy for the first time in his life. De Flers says : "I am happy to know you" . . .

Until today, I was still on the other side of the river. Neither *Poil de Carotte* nor *Histoires naturelles* had taken me across. Now, I feel that I have crossed.

Yesterday I went to sniff my glory in the country. The horse-chestnut trees wear a trimming of buds bought at the confectioner's. Leaves are fresh as little tongues; others have an oldish look, wrinkled as the forehead of a new-born babe; but the branches at the very tops of the trees are still as fine as hairs. The blossoms of the pear-tree are ready to go to a wedding.

Paris, seen from Meudon, looks like an immense stone-quarry.

"I have a hundred clippings," I say, "testifying to the success of *Plaisir de Rompre*."

Why do I say a hundred, when I know quite well there are not over seventy?

APRIL

A few more years, and I shall be full of illusions.

In the woods, the fir trees stick together, like priests.

Last night, at Mme. de Loynes's, the X-rays. . . . The footman . . . in a formidable voice, shouts: "Monsieur Renard!"

"I always expect Poil de Carotte to enter," says Mme. de Loynes.

I say good-evening to Sarah Bernhardt, who half-closes her little llama-eyes in order to make it look as though she did not see me. Decidedly, I am beginning to find this great actress insufferable, like everybody else. I shouldn't like God himself if he were not simple and unassuming. And, besides, she lives too hard to have the time to feel or think.

She gulps down life. It is a sort of gluttony, and unpleasant.

The X-rays, a childish plaything. They remind me of juvenile experiments in chemistry. It is a good deal less pretty than a ray of sunlight. Behind the screen, the professor says from time to time: "I discovered this . . ." and moves across it boxes, hands, arms, a little live dog . . .

The skeleton of Sarah Bernhardt's hand was photographed. She remained motionless on her knees for five minutes, always like a great artist . . .

If it is an entertainment, what a strange one! And there are no notes to take, these people have been emptied . . .

And this young woman, who is she? The daughter, or the governess of Mme. de Loynes, or of the little dogs? How much deference is to be shown her?

Oh, stay at home!

This morning, received a letter from my mother, saying that my father had an attack of suffocation, that he asked for a doctor himself, and that it's a congestion of the lungs and serious.

I am over thirty-three years of age, and it is the first time that I have been called upon to look fixedly at the possible death of a person loved. At first, it does not penetrate. I try to smile. A congestion of the lungs—that's nothing.

I do not think about my father. I think of the little details of death, and, as I foresee that I shall act foolishly, I say to Marinette:

"Now, don't go losing your head!"

I reserve the right of losing mine.

She tells me that I shall need black gloves and black buttons, and a band of crepe on my hat. I have no defenses against these mourning necessities, which I found ridiculous when others observed them. A father whom you seldom see, whom you seldom think about, is still something above you; and it is good to feel that there is someone higher, who may be a protector if need be, who is superior to you by reason of age, sense, responsibility.

With him dead, it seems to me that I shall resign myself to my place of chief; I shall be able to do what I like. Nobody will any longer have the right to judge me sternly. A very small child would be dejected if he knew that nobody would ever scold him. I was only beginning to love him.

Slight and frequent inclinations to weep. That kind of weeping is caused by the memory of universal tears that death calls forth.

He had a familiar gesture. He leaned his right elbow on the table, rested his cheek on his fingers, and, with the nail of his little finger, touched a receded tooth. I have inherited this tic. I have inherited evasive answers and the fear of enemas. My brother and sister have inherited other tics.

Between us, the words "filial" and "paternal" meant nothing. What bound us was a mixture of respect, astonishment, and fear. I was careful to say that he was different from others, and anxious to show that I was not afraid of him.

MAY

[Marinette goes to Chitry alone to help take care of JR's father.] Left alone, I think of Marinette as of a brand-new little woman whom I would be courting. And I also think of all the others.

Yesterday, after leaving her, I went a bit on foot with the hope of making some contact. But not one woman picked me up . . .

There you are! I, who long for adventures, wonder where I shall have my dinner.

Chaumot

"I feel stronger than last year," says papa.

He quivered with each fiery jab.

"Some people yell," he said. "It must relieve them. Perhaps I should yell."

He says of Papon, who has heart trouble:

"I hear he has a ridiculous fear of death."

Before swallowing a potion, he says:

"And what, according to you, is the virtue of this medicine?"

If you write to Jules Lemaître, write on the envelope "of the Académie Française." It will give pleasure to Jules Lemaître, and also to the postmistress of your village.

I no longer enjoy writing. I have made for myself too difficult a style.

Marinette says to papa:

"Did you have a bowel movement today?"

"Oh," says he, "every day can't be Sunday."

He looks at his nails and says:

"They're long, yellow, and black."

"Shall I cut them for you?" asks Marinette. And she cuts them and cleans them, while teasing: "Goodness, they're hard!"

"There are also the claws on the feet," says my father.

Marinette tells him she will cut them tomorrow.

Maman, in the kitchen, boiling with rage, says in a loud voice:

"You have one more to do. You should go now and clean up Papon."

She is approaching exasperation, and, since it is too early to get mad at Marinette, she flies at the maid: that girl, in stitches because the mistress of the house is being humiliated! The fact is that the master of the house never misses a shot. Hardly has maman left the room than she hears:

"Marie, bring me a cup of milk! Marie, a soft-boiled egg!"

"I am only good for emptying the pots that are handed to me," says maman.

Marinette tries to be tactful, but with little success. She says to the maid:

"Marie, this scarf should be washed."

And maman rushes forward: "I can wash it, since that's all I'm good for, besides emptying pots!"

Then suddenly she kisses Marinette, calling her: "My daughter! My dear daughter!" and, when she leaves, accompanies her to the street. She is very anxious to show herself informed of everything that's going on. She says:

"Yes, they produced a play by Jules. It is called *Le Désir de Rompre*. It was very successful. There was a lot of applause."

As Marinette passes a sponge over papa's face, maman, still in the kitchen, says:

"Oh, if only you would take advantage of his being sick to clean him up. He lives in shameful dirt. Thank heavens, at least I take care of his linen! All he has to do is open the closet and take out a shirt, a pair of drawers."

And papa no longer even laughs to himself. What is there between those two? A lot of little things, and nothing. He hates and despises her. Especially, he despises her, and I do believe he is also a little afraid of her.

As for her, she probably does not know. She is resentful because of her humiliations, of his obstinate silence. But if he said a word to her, she would cast herself upon his neck with a storm of tears, and, quickly, go repeating the word to the entire village. But it is thirty years since he has said a word.

Maurice took the revolver out of the drawer of the night table, saying he wanted to clean it. Papa, who feels well tonight, says:

"He said that, but he was lying. He is afraid that I'll kill myself. If I had a mind to kill myself I wouldn't use a tool that can only mutilate."

"Will you stop talking like that!" says Marinette.

"I'd go at it squarely and take my rifle."

"You'd do better to take an enema," I tell him.

Papa's intelligence is still slow and clear. My own, when I talk to him, no longer feels very sharp. I am always afraid of saying something *untrue*, and to say it badly, and he must think: "Why are they always talking about my son? I don't see anything special about him." He talks in a low voice, to spare his lung, and each of his so carefully husbanded words is painful to those who listen. As soon as maman opens the door, he stops. She comes in because she feels that he is about to say something she would like to know. Dragging her bad leg, she goes to the closet, opens it, touches the pile of linen, pretends to be looking for something, and takes nothing. She walks around the table, moves a newspaper. At last, she finds a cup and carries it away. She has heard nothing. As soon as the door is closed, papa, who was slowly walking about, completes his sentence in the same tone with which he started.

When the little peasant girls see us from a distance, they turn aside to smile.

JUNE

Papa keeps his mayor's sash in a little red box that once contained starched shirt-collars from the Bon Marché. When he has a marriage to perform, he takes the box to the mairie, places it on the table, and opens it. If they stand on tiptoe, the wedding pair and their witnesses can see the sash.

"That is enough," says papa.

He has never worn his sash; and there are people who are not sure that they are properly married.

They always want a happy ending! They would have Joan of Arc marrying Charles VII.

The bird alights on the rosebush not because of the rose, but because of the plant lice.

Men like my father respect only those that get rich, and admire only those that die poor.

Papa and the cupping. Six Bordeaux glasses are already lined up on the table, but the doctor brings real cupping-glasses and maman takes hers away.

Papa turns over on his right side. The doctor lights a piece of paper at a candle, puts the paper into a glass, and applies the glass to papa's back. Immediately, the skin swells up, in the manner of a lump on the forehead. The procedure repeated with six little glasses, and papa remains fifteen minutes with the little glasses on his back.

You may not find all this too interesting, but, after all, it does concern the back of my father.

Doctors will give utterance to certain technical words that surprise even themselves, after which they dare say nothing further.

That back with its russet tips of fire, its dark pattern of vesicatories, and its violet moons of cupping glasses, and way down, at the loins, an enormous freckle, and, still lower, a few long, sparse hairs, as fine as the hair on his head.

Empty buttocks with folds like the folds of empty sacks.

When he sleeps, the end of his nose, his cheekbones, and his finger-and-toe-nails turn purple. The blood no longer reaches them.

He always washed his face in a glass of water, using his cupped hands as a washcloth.

He always brushed his hair furiously.

He never wore either suspenders or finger rings.

He never put on a nightshirt, but wore his day shirt to bed.

He always pared his nails with a pocket knife.

He never went to bed without reading his paper or without blowing out his candle.

He never got into his trousers and his underdrawers separately.

I am a realist bothered by reality.

Nothing adds to your age like the death of a father. What? So I am now father Renard, and Fantec, from being a grandson, becomes a son.

The lady's companion who receives you with a hopeful smile: perhaps you are the one who will treat her with consideration.

After *Le Plaisir de Rompre* I thought I should work big. But how find, within myself, the material for three acts? Oh, for adventures, adventures!

And this Journal which distracts, amuses, and sterilizes me!

I write for an hour and immediately experience a depression; and even to write what I am writing here disgusts me.

Neither the Taines nor the Renans ever told us of these revulsions, these hidden sicknesses. Were they not acquainted with them? Did they have the pride not to complain, or the cowardice not to see clear in themselves?

Papa goes to the garden to sit under the hazel bushes, and does not notice that right by him there are a whitethroat's nest, a goldfinch's nest, a chaffinch's nest. How the sap has dried in him!

Half-past one. Death of my father.

One can say of him: "This was only a man, merely a mayor of a poor little village," and yet speak of his death as though it were the death of Socrates. I do not reproach myself for not having loved him enough. I do reproach myself for not having understood him.

After lunch, I was writing a few letters. The front doorbell rings. It is Marie, papa's little maid, come to tell me that he is asking for me. Why, she doesn't know. I stand up, just a little surprised. Marinette, perhaps more worried than I, says: "I'll go over." Without haste, I put on my shoes, blow up my tires.

Upon arriving at the house, I see maman in the street. She screams: "Jules! Oh! Jules!" and "Why did he lock himself in?" She looks like a madwoman. Still without excitement, I try to open the door. Impossible. I call; he doesn't answer. I guess nothing. I suppose that he suddenly felt worse, or that he is in the garden.

I ram the door with my shoulder, and the door gives.

Smoke and the smell of powder. And I find myself crying out: "Oh, papa, papa! What have you been doing? Well, there! Oh! Oh!" And still I don't believe it; he must be joking. And I don't believe his white face, his open mouth, and that blackness there, near the heart.

Borneau, who was returning from Corbigny, and is the next one to enter the room, says:

"He must be forgiven. That man was suffering too much."

Forgiven? For what? What an idea! I understand now, but I feel nothing. I go into the court, and I say to Marinette, who has lifted maman from the ground:

"It is finished. Come!"

She comes in, erect, pale, and looks sideways in the direction of the bed. She chokes, and opens the neck of her bodice. She is able to weep. She says, thinking of my mother:

"Don't let her in. She is out of her mind."

We both stay there. He is lying on his back, legs outstretched, the top of the body bent, head back, mouth and eyes open. Between his legs, his rifle; his walking stick between the bed and the wall: his hands, empty, have let go both stick and rifle. They are still warm, relaxed. A little above the waist, a black place, resembling a small extinguished fire.

No! He had not warned us. We talked often of death, but not of his. We should have needed Roman virtues. Perhaps he had them; not we.

On the whole, this death has added to my pride.

On June 21, at one o'clock, the coffin is taken out through the garden so that my mother and sister may not hear. People are waiting in the street . . .

The cemetery. The pit is there, in a corner, near the road . . . M. Billiard, in a clear voice, reads a written farewell, looking at me after each sentence . . .

They wait. Nothing more. I should like to explain the sense of this death, but there is nothing more.

All those people did not look too happy about taking part, out of decency, in this ceremony without a priest. No doubt this is the first civil interment in Chitry.

JULY

I take him with me, fishing, everywhere.

Marinette, who is supposed to cheer me up, weeps.

He had seemed part of his garden, like the trees.

Sometimes, in a macabre imitation, I stop in the middle of the road and open my mouth the way his was open on the bed.

For the first time since he was buried, I passed near the cemetery. I stopped automatically. So he is there, a few steps away, on the other side of the wall, lying on his back and already worm-eaten.

He had shown no decrepitude, so that he seems to me to have killed himself in full strength, a strength greater than mine.

My laziness feeds on his death. My only inclination is to contemplate the picture that struck so terribly at my eyes.

His cemetery. Poppies, high grasses where the larks will find shelter. A long worm comes out of the loosened earth. A few ants. Every instant I forget that he is there, that I am walking over him.

No matter how far life may take me, death will bring me back to his side.

We made, as it were, a little cage for him out of pine wood.

I can already reserve my share of earth.

Seated in the narrow shade of the wall, I try to remember what he was like.

I wear out his memory.

Flowers on a grave turn ugly, like old signboards above pot-houses.

His grave does not sadden me, no doubt because he is there. But when, from the road, I look at the house in which he killed himself, his house, and I don't see him, from the back, sitting on his wall with his arms crossed, and I don't see his white beard under his straw hat, I am sad that he is no longer there.

Maurice says to me:

"One of these days, I'll fool you. I'll sit in his place on the wall."

And suppose he had missed? Suppose he had just damaged himself? Suppose he had not had the strength to take that second shot? Suppose he had screamed at me: "Finish me off!" What would I have done?

Would I have been brave enough to take his rifle, or to choke him with a hug?

He slept sitting on his bed, his nostrils open, his kerchief of red, white and blue madras knotted around his head, his pince-nez on his nose, his hands on his belly, and, in his hands, the paper *l'Eclair* fallen on the comforter.

After a visit from the doctor, when we were discussing his condition, my mother came close to listen: still giving the impression of listening at a keyhole.

Mocking, he would say to the doctor:

"I have just eaten a bacon-and-parsley omelet."

Already I have to darken my eyes to be able to see him.

Oh, not now! But I have a feeling that, later on, in a moment of utter disgust, in what Baudelaire calls "dull lack of curiosity," I will do as he did. Little empty cartridge-shell, looking at me like an eye put out!

Never let it be said: "His father was braver than he!"

My father had a heart, but his heart was not a home.

For a while, his death made me feel uprooted.

Here, after someone has died, the straw in his mattress is burned; it is a sanitary measure. The cloth, of course, is kept, and the rest of the bedding is not touched.

Philippe said to my father:

"You're the same age as my father."

"Oh? and what age would he be?"

Philippe did some figuring and said:

"He would be a hundred and seven years old."

Without appearing to joke, papa said:

"Perhaps you get old faster when you're dead."

A rock carries moss. My father had no visible softness, and never said thank you.

My father. The next day I had to leave the table in order to go away and weep. It was the first time, in the twenty hours that I had sat by him. Floods of tears came to my eyes; I had not been able to squeeze out one before.

What a beautiful death! I think that if he had killed himself in front of me I should have let him go ahead. One should not lessen the merit of his act. He killed himself, not because he suffered too much, but because he did not want to live otherwise than in good health.

He should have told me. We could have discussed his death in the manner of Socrates and his friends. Perhaps he thought of it.

But I know very well I would have been stupid. I would have said: "You're crazy! Leave me alone, let's talk about something else."

I am less afraid of death than I was. Already, I am less afraid of thunderstorms. (It isn't true.)

A magnificent example! And no duel: I shall kill myself whenever I please. There is lead in my life: the buckshot of my father's death.

The magpie fluttered about, dressed up as a sister of charity.

Those pieces in verse are empty shells, inside of which you put Sarah Bernhardt.

AUGUST

The death of my father makes me feel as though I had written a beautiful book.

SEPTEMBER

Return to Paris. My father and I did not love each other outwardly. We did not hang together by our branches: we loved each other by our roots.

How annoying to be in mourning! Every moment, you must remind yourself that you are sad.

When laziness makes us miserable, it has the same value as work.

OCTOBER

Verlaine, his last verses. He was no longer writing: he was playing at jacks with words.

Mallarmé writes intelligently like a madman.

NOVEMBER

Guitry. Never will I dare read to that man my naïve and silly little play.

Last night, read to Guitry, in his dressing room [*Le Pain de Ménage*] during two intermissions. Door closed to everyone . . .

I stumble a bit. From Guitry, nothing. A disconcerting silence, except for a "Oh, that's good!" Then: "Let's stop here. It is exquisite, delicious. One feels in the presence of something beautiful." . . .

He really seems caught. I am in a state of delight. And yet, at bottom, I was sure.

I read what I write as though I were my mortal enemy.

DECEMBER

It is in the gentle climate of this woman that I should like to live and die.

One must admire the genius of Musset: his defects were only those of his period.

Music is an art that frightens me. I feel as though I were in a tiny boat on immense waves. What revolts me against music, of which I know nothing, is that little provincial justices of the peace are crazy about it. What can those people be crazy about?

Alphonse Daudet is dead . . .

We are too preoccupied with death. We should not take note when it passes; it might come less often. It has no importance whatsoever.

A sort of dream that I dream on my feet, as though my unconscious were chasing out my conscious self and putting itself in its place. I don't know them, those images that so suddenly appear. And since I can't deny their existence, since they are there, in me, I must believe that they belong to another self, and that I am double.

Yesterday, did not think of my father. If I think of him today, it is only to reproach myself with not having done so yesterday.

Cyrano. Flowers, nothing but flowers, all the flowers in the world to our great dramatic poet! . . . The friendship of Rostand consoles me for having been born too late to be a member of the circle of Victor Hugo.

[After the opening night of *Cyrano de Bergerac.* In the dressing room of Coquelin, who created the role.]

Sarah Bernhardt enters.

"Rostand, Rostand! Where is Rostand?"

"He has returned to the Renaissance [the theater where Sarah is playing]," I say.

"You are stupid," she says. And I am not sure that it is meant pleasantly. Then she says:

"I managed to see the last act. How beautiful! Act by act, my son kept me informed, in my dressing room. I hurried my dying. At last, I am here. And in what a state! . . . Look at my tears! Look! Look! I am weeping."

And everyone feels like saying: "Why, no, madame! I assure you." Then, she pounces upon Coquelin, takes his head in both hands like a soup tureen, and she bends over him, and she drinks him, and she eats him.

"Coq!" she says. "O great Coq!"

At last, Rostand! And she takes him for herself alone, again by the head, but this time like a cup of champagne. . . .

"You have written me a letter that is a masterpiece," Rostand tells me. "If you ever speak ill of me, I shall publish it." . . .

"I haven't witnessed so much glory since the war," says a military man.

"But I thought we had lost the war," I say.

1898

*I turn home, my heart filled with anguish because
I have watched the sun set and heard the birds sing, and
because I shall have had so few days on this earth I love,
and there are so many dead before me.*

Le Pain de Ménage is produced with great success.

JANUARY

Failure is not our only punishment for laziness: there is also the success of others.

Rostand has added nothing to men like Banville and Gautier but the art of never being boring.

[Hughes Le Roux] . . . And this extraordinary and useless man makes a pretty contrast with Mallarmé, who is gentle, who is modest, who thinks before speaking, who would prefer to think without speaking, and whose coat is without a stain.

[Hervieu]. In order to be in everything, he works like a brute, instead of lazying around like an intelligent man.

[*La Ville Morte* by d'Annunzio]. It is poetry as gold is a precious metal–by convention.

Old woman, your eyes are like the reflection of a star in the water of a wagon rut.

A line of verse is always to a certain extent a cage for thought.

"You are working?"
  "I am trying to work; which is much more difficult."

The child. When dinner is over, I run my hand through his hair, I pinch his ear, just to make sure he is there.

I am a man continually astonished, each instant just fallen from the moon.

FEBRUARY

Unpleasant things make me very unhappy, and yet I prefer them to others.

I was brought up by a library.

I never noticed that the compliments made to me were not sincere.

MARCH

Mallarmé, untranslatable, even into French.

Le Pain de Ménage . . . In the satisfaction my friends show, something troubles me, as though they might be gay because it is not too, too good.

At the *Figaro*, this evening. Veber:

"Well, Renard, have you digested your success?"

"What about you?" I ask him.

After the first few lines, I feel easy. I am no longer the author, and I let myself be charmed, and I applaud with the public, who follow the play as though they had written it. [Marthe] Brandès and Guitry tell me:

"We had to force them to calm down, or we could not have spoken a line."

Three or four curtain calls, and my name dropped into the midst of all that as though into a pond of charming frogs.

Now I am on the spot! Without this fresh success, I might have written five passable acts. Now I have license to write only the marvelous . . .

All the same, I did not dare kiss Brandès.

APRIL–Chaumot

Trees with the rough hide of a rhinoceros.

At the cemetery. I try to imagine the horrible thing that my father's face is now, and I feel the grimace made by my own face.

If I am no longer young, I should like to know at what hour of what day my youth left me.

The duck tries to jump over a wall and go through a hedge. Halfway up the wall, she falls back heavily. She does not insist: she goes to fetch the drake. Together, their heads held straight up, they examine the wall, look for an opening in the hedge. From time to time, they desist, go around by the field, cut a little grass, and come back.

The duck gets half-way into the hedge; but it is too thick: she gives up the idea.

They make the turn of the meadow, wasting their day and mine.

And their jerky bows.

It is a confused act. It would take a comic playwright to straighten it out.

The cold shadow of spring, broken by sound, by wind.

Like the soil, my courage needs rain.

Do not ask me to be kind; just ask me to act as though I were.

A pale sunlight—the kind of sunlight needed by trees that have as yet no shading leaves.

What calm! I hear all my thoughts.

When I give a hundred-franc bill, I give the dirtiest one.

I look at Fantec. He is nearly ten years old. When he is fifteen I shall not be forty, and there is almost nothing in common between us.

And I don't care that he should either admire me or read my books.

Don't tell a woman she is pretty. Tell her that she is not like the others, and all her avenues will be open to you.

An asparagus stalk with a serpent's, an adder's head.

If you want to please women, tell them the things you would not want other men to tell your wife.

MAY

Inspiration is perhaps only the joy of writing; it does not precede writing.

At the Salon . . . where I had not been for ten years. Only the statue of Balzac by Rodin attracts my eye. Seen from a three-quarter view, at twenty meters, its attitude is striking. And those hollow eyes, that grimacing face, that narrow forehead, that man swaddled and entangled in his working garment, that is something. You could say of this statue what Mme. Victorine de Chatenay said of Joubert: "A soul that by accident had met a body and was trying to get along as best it could."

But everything else! . . . Upon going out of the Salon, you are pleased with anything your eye may light upon.

Pierre Loti. It was with an almost religious air that Antoine told us: "Loti is coming this evening."

Rings, a tie-pin that is too large, too golden: it looks like a royal crown. A young, too young appearance, a little faded.

"We meet for the first time," he says, "but we have written to each other. It is a long time since you have published anything. Besides, I am not au courant. I read nothing. It's ridiculous."

So he still has that affectation of pretending he reads nothing. But how young he looks! I don't understand it [Loti was then 48]. I should not have known him from his pictures.

"My face changes so!" he says. "I never look the same two days running."

There must be another reason, which I am not aware of . . .

He laughs, with a strange and charming laugh. His lips draw back from fine teeth, and the rest of his face remains immovable. Then his lips come together, and they look as though they were afraid of touching each other . . .

He insists in a special way upon being presented to "Madame Jules Renard." No doubt to him she is a new woman, and from every new woman he expects something. Marinette, embarrassed, barely looks at him. But she sees at once what I did not see.

An exquisite and elaborate courtesy forces me into an awkward show of manners. A few white hairs in the mustache. The hair of a young man. Large, slightly faded ears and eyes—how describe them?

"But he is made up! Made up like a woman," Marinette tells me after we have left him. "His eyelashes are made up, his eyes are made up, his hair shines, and his lips are painted. He doesn't even dare close his mouth; and those white hairs in his mustache—those are to make you think that the rest is natural."

I saw nothing, Frère Yves.

JUNE–Chaumot

Michelet tries too hard to poetize nature—something she does not need. It does not help to overdo her, and, in spite of his efforts, she escapes him. Read this sentence addressed to a group of peasants: "That ringing voice of the lark, full of power, gives the signal to the harvesters. It is time to go, the father said: don't you hear the lark?" The peasants might be surprised. Not one of them has ever been given such a signal: not one would have obeyed it.

Carried away by his words, he was no longer capable of seeing. Incomparable when he describes a storm at sea, he exaggerates the lark.

JULY

No one will ever stop me from being moved when I look at a field, when I walk up to my knees through oats that spring up behind me. What thought is as fine as this blade of grass?

I don't give a straw for "my country" as a whole: my local country moves me to tears. The German emperor cannot take this blade of grass from me.

Seated by the edge of the canal, facing the cemetery, I read to the memory of my father.

How superior to their own life is our memory of the dead! It has no leftover bits and pieces.

There is not only the moon. There are also evil and mysterious winds that dry out a single branch in the middle of a tree and cause it to die.

My father's contempt for people who write. To write is to indulge in talk, and he cared only for political talk. I should have risen in his esteem only if I could have told him: "I had dinner with Deschanel [at the time, President of the Chamber]." Oh, he would not have jumped with pride, but he would have put something comical and astonished into his "Ah!"

My style, full of tours de force that no one notices.

I like solitude, even when I am alone.

Our egoism is so excessive that, in a storm, we believe the thunder to be directed only at us.

What is difficult is not to be good but not to be ashamed of it. Not to say to oneself: "How can I, who am currently reading Pascal, be a good husband and a good papa, and go walking on Sundays with my wife and offspring?" What is difficult is not to think: "If someone should see me!"

From her window, my mother sees Marinette approaching. She goes and sits in the middle of the kitchen and begins to cry, so that Marinette may find her in tears.

"Goodness! What's the matter, maman?"

"I have thoughts."

We can't find out about what. We can guess they are thoughts of suicide. Certainly, something is bothering her. Furious over not having been invited to my lecture on Michelet, she was saying to Marie Pierry: "You're going to get a bad reputation, mixing with those people! You know the priests don't like that sort of thing!" To Marinette she said:

"I heard it was ever so beautiful!"

Through Philippe, she learns that I ate two or three sour cherries.

"Oh, I'm not surprised! He loved them so when he was little! He used to get them all over him. There! Bring him a whole basketful! Poor Jules, how happy he'll be!"

All day, the woods hold in their branches a little of the night.

I don't give a fig for intelligence: I should be satisfied with a lot of instinct.

Death is comforting: it delivers us from the thought of death.

AUGUST

Having no future, my father was not curious about what mine would be.

First you love nature. It is only much later that you reach man.

A stupid faith cannot but displease God.

Let us stay at home: there we are decent. Let us not go out: our defects wait for us at the door, like flies.

She says to Ragotte:

"You're like me, you can live all you like with gentry, you talk as bad one time as another, always in patois."

"Nobody would understand me if I talked different," says Ragotte.

The houses look into the street through their open, illuminated doors. All the light comes out into the street.

There is nothing like a disciple to show us our faults.

The best among us has a few small murders to reproach himself with.

Why should it he more difficult to die, that is, to go from life to death, than it is to be born, that is, to go from death to life?

There cannot be on the one side form, and on the other, matter. A bad style is an imperfect thought.

I turn home, my heart filled with anguish because I have watched the sun set and heard the birds sing, and because I shall have had so few days on this earth I love, and there are so many dead before me.

OCTOBER

Pigeons. Their flight has the sound of the smothered laughter of girls, of nuns in a convent.

An admission: work creates a slightly complacent satisfaction. Laziness, on the other hand, gives rise to a state of anxiety that brings us out of ourselves: the mind may owe to it some of its most subtle perceptions.

I have never experienced a sincere emotion at the theatre, except at my own plays.

One could say of almost all literature that it is too long.

I want to create a style for myself as clear to the eyes as a spring morning.

NOVEMBER

God does not believe in our God.

I always feel like saying to music: "It isn't true! You lie!"

DECEMBER

The moon spreads winter. All the cold falls from this moon that glitters in the sky like a piece of ice.

A pox on the bourgeois! It is only artists who can appreciate a meal of hot food, wholesome and well-cooked, white linen, sharp knives, a good wood fire and a lamp that gives light.

The moon spreads a fine, even snow over the roofs.

1899

I am not content with intermittent life:
I must have life at each instant.

JANUARY–Chaumot

Winter trees, drawn with a pen. The horse-chestnut raises its bayonets. The dry hair of the willow is all tousled.

The lips of the water sucking the ice.

The silky sound of the reeds.

The shepherd with his sheep looks like a church with its village.

Barrès plays on reason the way others play on the flute.

I no longer read anything but selected pieces from French literature. I only wish I could have selected them myself.

Anatole France. He is very pleasant, like a man whose face is always caught in the door, and who doesn't want you to squeeze.

FEBRUARY

At night, I often think I hear the cock crow. The next morning, I ask Philippe if he heard it. He says he did not, and this troubles me.

To describe a peasant, one should not use words he would not understand.

I feel that someone guides me.

What will save me is a taste I have, a sort of minor taste for saintliness.

The cat is the life of furniture.

MARCH

I was born with two wings, one of them broken.

Spiders draw plans of capital cities.

APRIL

For a writer who has been working, to read is like getting into a carriage after a toilsome walk.

The gentle melancholy of working on Sunday, when the others are loafing.

I am not content with intermittent life: I must have life at each instant.

Baïe says to her mother: "At the fair I saw a cow as beautiful as you."

Poil de Carotte. I was never able to make a single decisive gesture without convulsing my brother with laughter. Hence my humble, colorless life.

I do not have a tower, I have a notebook of ivory.

Romantics are people who have never seen the wrong side of anything.

Go out! Fine weather lost is never found again.

When I got married, I brought my young wife into my family. My father looked around for something to do in her honor. He decided he would replace a few of the tiles on his house with new ones; then he gave up the idea.

I pick myself up as easily as I fall. Light as a spider, my soul climbs up on a thread.

In an instant, the mind travels over immense dream countries, while the eyes go over reality like tortoises.

I write down thoughts for when I am dead. They are of no use to me while I am alive. I even forget to think them.

Unsightly as a piece of paper in a meadow.

All the same, little by little I give up a great many things that I cannot have.

MAY

Sarah's popular Saturday afternoons . . .

Sarah, who has a piece in verse to recite, is as feverish as though she were playing *Phèdre* for the first time . . .

Mendès says to Guitry, elegantly: "The prose pieces of Jules Renard have become part of you." Rostand arrives. He is decidedly a great man. He offers only that hand which holds his cane. If spoken to, he barely answers. I find all this perfectly proper, because he puts himself out for me.

Guitry recites. Tristan Bernard comes to look for me. "Come along, Renard! Guitry is taking his third curtain call."

Sarah, icy, pretends not to know that everything Guitry has been reciting is by me.

There are storytellers and writers. You can tell any story you like; you cannot write whatever you like: you write only yourself.

Soon the horse will be something as strange as the giraffe.

JUNE–Chaumot

At the bottom of all patriotism there is war: that is why I am no patriot.

A walk in the country. I pass by the cemetery. I dare not think of what is left of my father behind that wall, a few feet away. I move on. The entire length of a flowery path, my soul toys with thoughts of death. Every moment, I turn my head and try to see La Gloriette. I wonder if it is on a higher level than the château, than the school, if it runs a greater risk than another house of being struck by lightning. This idiotic fear of storms, even on the finest days, keeps me as it were on the alert. Thanks to it, I am a little less lazy.

I walk among the wheat, which is fine this year. The north wind is good for it. The south wind would have burnt off the flowers. My cane, which I carry behind my back, sweeps down the ears of wheat. Poppies run before me. I come to the wood, cool, silent, and holy as a church, and enter it by a wide avenue that cuts it in two. The chill tickles my nostrils, and suddenly I feel myself to be lightly clad.

Who is coming toward me, over there, through the trees? No one.

Who is walking over the leaves? Souls without bodies.

Birds made of sunlight have alighted on the ground, and hide and move about with the movement of the leaves.

Vitai lampada tradunt. The wind, soul of the trees, is passed on from one to the other.

Happily, at the end of the avenue, I find daylight. Everything in me lights up.

I hear the swish of a scythe in the grass. I see it in the distance; it seems to be gently waltzing. Flies sting me. The weather—no: my mood is about to change.

Behind me, the cuckoo, mysterious, invisible, of ill fame, sings. It is accused of placing its eggs, one by one, in the nests of a white-throat, a robin, a nightingale, a wagtail, a thrush, a blackbird. Is that a crime? And what about you? Don't you ever leave your young in other people's beds? But you do not have the honesty to sing out "Cuckoo!" in warning.

What? A purse. No. It's a mole that a mower has killed and thrown on the path.

I can guess that a hay wagon has passed here. Many a bramble has nipped up a stalk as it passed, and is holding on to it.

From this first walk I bring back a wild rose, an indigent rose possessing only a thin dress, and no petticoats.

Hayricks like a little village of huts arranged in rows, and the moon walking through its streets.

Yesterday, anniversary of my father's death. Without Marinette, I should have forgotten it.

My mother, who is in bed, has the priest say a mass. So, three or four old women listen to a priest praying for my father.

Marinette and I bring him a rather heavy wreath made out of glazed earthenware.

It is less cruel never to visit the dead than to cease going after a while.

I have my faults like everyone; only I don't get any good out of them.

Those moments when you feel you want to read something truly beautiful. The eyes make a tour of the library, and there is nothing. Then you decide to take no matter what, and it is full of beautiful things.

When I used to see my father walking from one window to the other, bent, silent, his hands behind his back, his look deep, I used to ask myself: "What is he thinking about?" Today I know, because I walk about in exactly the same manner, with the same air, and I can answer in all certainty: "Nothing."

JULY

Baïe places a snail beside a tortoise, to see what they will say to each other.

Bells live in the air, like birds.

The air, at midday, burns and hums.

To think is not enough; you must think of something.

I am not struck by things: I remember them.

Our life seems like a trial run.

Their language is full of little pennyworth images that amuse them.

Style is the habit, the second nature of thought.

If man had the power of adding to nature, he would give thorns to the serpent.

AUGUST

Francis Jammes fusses too much. Art is something sterner and does not tolerate over-refinement. Simple does not mean bloodless.

Meadows are meadows, but fields are earth.

SEPTEMBER

The yellowing leaves make the trees look as though they were ripe.

On the hunt . . . The country seems inhabited only by oxen. I ask: "Why is that farm in that spot rather than in another?" Philippe tells me it is near a spring that never runs dry. So that is the explanation.

OCTOBER

Return to Paris. The setting sun is pink like the interior of a seashell.

The wind claps in the night like a black sheet.

All summer long I have lived on my intellectual dividends. Oh, my tastes are simple! All my mind needs is to make both ends meet.

They believe themselves to be men of action because they take the best seats in railway carriages.

At Guitry's. The pleasure of placing my hand in the wide palm of this man. Brandès still has her pretty figure. She puts much wine in the glasses and much red meat on the plates.

We read Molière. Guitry reads from *Le Misanthrope* with an intelligence of which his ordinary public has no inkling. What a poverty of images in Molière, but what bitter eloquence!

NOVEMBER

Poil de Carotte. I read it to Antoine. Even before the scene in the barn, I hear: "It's a marvel." After that, I read with more assurance, that is, less well . . .

"It's a marvel," repeats Antoine . . . "I have seldom heard anything like it. I should not have thought you could make that out of *Poil de Carotte.* You will have a hundred performances."

"You're not joking?"

"I am incapable of joking."

"And you are ready to play Lepic?"

"I should say so!"

I notice that I have already put on my hat. Solemnly, I take it off. That should have pleased Antoine.

How quickly joy becomes tiring! I shouldn't want to be too happy for anything in the world. Joy affects the heart like burning ice.

DECEMBER

Go to meet a poet with a few of his verses on your lips.

One should have the courage to prefer the intelligent man to the very nice man.

Jammes does not understand the poetry of the things we find unpleasing in nature: he is too much of a honey-pot.

If I had done something different from what I am capable of doing, you would see how bad it would be!

Irony does not dry up the grass; it just burns off the weeds.

Poil de Carotte. Reading at Guitry's. After the scene of the servant, he says: "It is beautiful." At the scene of the suicide: "That is good." I read to the end, pushing a bit. When I am through, I see tears in his eyes.

"It is beautiful," he says.

"And now," I say, "criticisms."

"Wait a minute! First of all, you must absolutely give that to the Comédie-Française. I, only I, can play M. Lepic. His kindness." (I think to myself: M. Lepic is not a kind man; he is a man with moments of poignant compassion.)

Guitry insists. I reply that I cannot.

"Criticisms," I say.

"The public will be all choked up: it isn't good to go beyond a certain emotion. . . . *Poil de Carotte* must not sound like a revenge by Jules Renard."

1900

*I, I, not an enthusiast? A few notes of music, the sound of
flowing water, the wind in the leaves, and my poor heart runs
over with tears, with real tears—yes, yes!*

This year, with the overwhelming success of *Poil de Carotte* as a play, JR attains real
fame. The play has a long run in Paris, is given all over France. JR receives the cross
(ribbon) of the Legion of Honor.

JANUARY

Guitry will play the part of the old grenadier in *L'Aiglon*. He is pale
with emotion.

"It is magnificent," he says.

"Rostand is a genius," I say.

"Yes! To do something as prodigious as *L'Aiglon* one must be sick.
Capus can't get away with saying it's just music."

Rostand has written a letter to a Cabinet minister, M. Leygues, on
my behalf [to obtain the Legion of Honor for JR]. Mme. Rostand
quotes sentences of it to Marinette, who repeats them to me. They

bring tears to my eyes, and make my heart feel full, myself already decorated.

The minister must have thought he was mad.

Poor Rostand is most unhappy. He thinks that *L'Aiglon* is boring. His very life has become a burden. He doesn't go to sleep before six o'clock in the morning; and every day his doctor gives him an injection of I know not what.

When I get home, Marinette tells me that it's all set. Mme. Rostand brought a little box of ribbons and a small diamond cross. On my part, amazement. No joy: I have doubts. Marinette reassures me. In *Le Temps*, *Les Débats*, nothing. *La Presse* says that I'm not in.

I send Marinette to Rostand's. There is a telegram from Franc-Nohain: he has seen Lapauze, who has no definite information.

So there we are. That is the best we have been able to do in this foolish juncture, with which I am, finally, fed up. My brother is here, sitting in the armchair and making the stupid remarks of a wiseacre. He knew it all along!

Through the window, I see people stopping on the other side of the street, looking this way. I peer down, and perceive a white horse: the carriage of the Rostands. Mme. Rostand comes in, looking a little grave.

"My poor friend, I have bad news, I'd rather tell you at once. I could weep. It was sure, and then at the last moment you were replaced by Morand, who is a friend of Loubet [then President of France]. Rostand is furious."

She gets warm as she says it. I feel very little emotion, and I don't know why the corner of my eye is moist.

"He will come to see you," she says. "He will explain. We'll know the details."

Really, I am not at all upset. I notice that she is wearing a dress of black silk, and a spring-like hat, and that she is tired. She feels that I am taking it well. I have the pale, interesting air of a newly-delivered mother.

Gémier congratulates me, rather limply, on having honored the Legion of Honor, opens my overcoat, sees nothing, and makes the mistake of apologizing.

They talk of my *authority*. Frankly, they annoy me. I have a reputation for reserve. I can no longer say a flattering thing without its taking on proportions that impinge on my sincerity. I shall no longer go anywhere, or say anything nice to anyone.

Maurice. Six o'clock in the evening. On behalf of Mlle. Neyrat, the Society for the Protection of Animals has sent me a Pomeranian. The children are playing with him, and he has been given the name of Papillon when an employee from the State Railways comes to tell us that Maurice has fallen into a faint and cannot be revived. I feel ill-humored; I do not think of death. I remember papa's fainting spells. I'll bring him around, give him a shake, and tell him that when you are ill you go to bed.

Rue de Châteaudun, No. 42. People in the vestibule. A small, fat man, the red ribbon of the Legion in his lapel, comes running, says: "Your poor brother is very low," then, in my ear, so that Marinette may not hear: "He is dead." The word means nothing.

"Well," I say, "where is he?" . . .

He is stretched out on a pale green sofa, his mouth open, a knee bent, his head on a city directory, in the attitude of a tired man. He reminds me of my father. On the floor, spots of water, a rag.

He is dead, but it does not penetrate.

All I feel is a sort of anger at death and its imbecile tricks.

I write telegrams on bits of paper, and I do believe that, on account of all those people around, I write badly to make it look as though I were trembling; because it still does not penetrate . . .

They take me to his office . . . Steam-heated, the temperature went as high as 20 degrees [68 F.]. The steam pipe was right behind him. He had often said: "They're going to kill me, with their heating system!"

The ambulance arrives . . . Little by little, Maurice Renard will be replaced by big brother Felix [his counterpart in JR's works]. Then it will penetrate . . .

Marinette and I sit with him until four o'clock in the morning.

His life has passed into the furniture, and the slightest creak sends shivers through us.

We seem to hurry, a little surprised to be alive.

Visitors. Comrades come to pay their respects . . . A poor little woman, passing the door with her milk box, stops, sets down her box, says: "I'm sorry! I didn't know." She kneels, says a short prayer, blesses herself, and goes.

Wednesday. Trip to Chitry. People are surprised that maman and my sister have permitted a non-religious interment. They say: "It is Jules's doing." I didn't really care. But Philippe and Pierre Bertin helped me: Maurice had always told them that he wanted to be buried like his father.

Ragotte tells me that she was in Pazy, when a woman who had come from Corbigny asked her: "Have you heard the news?" "No." "M. Jules is dead. They're bringing him home tomorrow." She returned home in a hurry; she couldn't walk fast enough. She was saying to herself: "Such a nice lady, and she was always making over him! If only, now, it had been M. Maurice!" When Philippe set her straight she felt relieved. She had carried me, dead, in her heart for three kilometers. For some reason, I derive from this a certain idiotic satisfaction, as though it had made me interesting.

During the night of the wake I asked him several times, almost out loud, to forgive me for having been unfeeling toward him. But, except at bottom, he hadn't been very brotherly, either.

The curé had hoped until the last moment to be called in. He put off mass until eleven o'clock.

FEBRUARY

Poil de Carotte. Rehearsal. Antoine . . . directs them with an intelligence that makes me feel so modest, I don't dare contradict him a single time.

"You are indispensable," I tell him.

"I'll get there," he says, "but it annoys me sometimes to have to do two jobs at the same time." He says to "his" women [the part of Poil de Carotte was played by a young woman]:

"Don't touch the text. If the author wrote that, he had his reasons" . . .

When it is over, I thank him with childlike joy. Guitry is all diction, Antoine all action, by which I mean the fire, the life, the naked sense of the lines.

MARCH

Poil de Carotte. Rehearsal. . . . Antoine doesn't know his part properly, and then all of a sudden the thing goes off and nothing stops it. Tears run down the face of Poil de Carotte, streaking his rouge. He has a terrible face, the face of a mother's killer. And you feel that Antoine is holding back, that he will be much better. Maupin cries because Mme. Lepic is so harsh, but she adds:

"It is nothing. It's just play-acting."

Marinette is no longer afraid of anything. She frightens me a little. But I feel relieved. I have extracted from Poil de Carotte the essence I wanted . . .

Marinette in the dressing-room of Maupin, listening to life stories. "They're nice, those little actresses!" says Marinette.

I go to the theatre on foot . . . Desprès (Poil de Carotte) is pale with emotion; Antoine is nervous. He barely listens when I tell him something. I stay in his dressing room.

I walk, look vaguely around. I touch things. At last I hear the curtain go down, and noises. Then strange faces arrive, Antoine, who kisses Desprès and says, restraining himself: "It's a great success!" Desprès, her wig off and beaming, tells me: "You're the one we should ask if he's happy!"

The beautiful faces that come, lighted up by smiles, softened by tears. Guitry: "It is even better than what one expected of you." Brandès: "I am so happy! What a great artist you are!" Marinette, overflowing with joy, Descaves, Courteline, a little dry, Porto-Riche who nods his head, Capus who tells me: "It's top drawer," and makes me feel badly about the unkind remarks I made about *his* play.

"I did nothing," Antoine says to Marinette. "He did everything. He brought me a stack of notes."

At the office of *La Revue Blanche*, Mirbeau draws me into a corner and asks if I want him to set me up as a candidate at the Académie Goncourt. If I do, it's as good as done. Hennique, he says, leaped upon the idea.

I answer—that I'll answer, and that I do not want to go against Descaves. I'll think about it.

L'Aiglon. A prodigy, a little lengthy, of virtuosity. It crushes you with its beauty and, a little, with its tedium. You admire without emotion. Incredible and banal . . . It is as though you were in front of a beautiful waterfall: after a while you want to leave.

In Sarah's dressing room [Sarah played the title part], Rostand calls me to him. We embrace, but, I am not prepared. I have no emotion ready. In spite of the words "genius" and "way above *Cyrano*," I feel that I barely succeed in being pleasant.

In this somber prodigy, the greatest lustre fell upon Guitry. Interminable applause followed his first long passage. Sarah was smiling and seemed tiny, pocket-sized.

After demands from the public that refused to end, Rostand came out and took two bows. Tomorrow, if he wishes, he will be king of France.

MAY—Chaumot

Maman. Marinette talks me into going to see her. My heart beats a little faster, out of uneasiness. She is in the passageway. She immediately begins to cry. The little maid doesn't know where to look. She kisses me at length. I give her one kiss.

She takes us into papa's room and kisses me again, saying:

"I'm so glad you came! Why don't you come now and then? Oh, my God! I'm so miserable!"

I answer nothing and go into the garden. She says:

"Go and see the poor garden! The chickens don't leave a grain in it."

I am hardly outside before she falls at Marinette's feet and thanks her for having brought me. She says:

"I have only him left. Maurice never looked at me, but he came to see me."

She wants to give me a silver fork and spoon. She offers a clock to Marinette. One day she had said to Baïe: "At Saint-Etienne I saw such a pretty little penknife for you, I almost bought it."

It was more than a year since I had seen her. I find her not so much aged as fat and flabby. It is still the same face, with that something disquieting behind the features.

Nobody laughs or cries as easily as she does.

I say good-bye without turning my head.

At my age, I swear nobody affects me as much as she does.

Elections . . . I find that my name has been placed on the lists. And here I am bothered again, the way I always am when there is a question of niceties. I could tell M. de Talon that I do not admit of this way of using my name without consulting me first; or I could accept. It is not so simple.

Do I or don't I wish to be a municipal councillor? Yes, I do. But I should like to be sure of going over on the first ballot . . .

People talk in corners, in low voices. Last night, meeting of the councillors. M. de Talon takes them out to drink. He tells them that, without me, the school will fall to nothing.

This morning, on the road, I cross the mayor of Chitry. He is returning from planting his potatoes. He walks under his hod. He looks like the poorest man in the village. It wouldn't be bad if he were re-elected on the strength of that fact.

Ragotte would be vexed if Philippe were not elected. She likes him to be "regarded."

Elections of May 6. Sunday. Elected by 31 votes out of 50.

All morning, I watch, from the bench [in front of his house] . . .

After lunch, I make up my mind to go to the mairie, which until then frightened me a little. People stand up, I shake hands, but badly, I feel . . .

The moment comes to close the polls. The checkers settle down. The box is emptied.

It is over. All the outgoing councillors are re-elected, plus me. I say to all:

"Gentlemen, I invite you, those who have voted for and those who have voted against me, to have a glass of beer."

Almost everyone comes. I do not count them, but thirty-seven bottles are scattered on the ground, like small spent cannons. If we were to vote now, I should have ten additional votes.

The township of Chaumot is of such overwhelming importance that the regional papers do not even mention its municipal elections. Those of Paris, *La Presse*, *L'Evénement*, *Le Matin*, announce my election, but at Corbigny, four kilometers from here, no one suspects it. It is true that I had the foresight to notify Paris myself.

A flame—is it the last?—on the hearth; a rose—it is the first—in a glass of water.

JUNE

At bottom, the curé of Chitry was deeply humiliated because I never returned the call he had hesitated three months to pay me . . .

"You see?" he says. "He is ambitious, your Renard! He came to Chaumot to look after his election. He wants titles. Not being able to belong to the Académie, he has himself elected municipal councillor. He has certain illusions about the local people. I have talked to him. I know what he is: a dreamer (he smiles): a poet. He is proud, too. He was offered the job of deputy to M. de Talon; but he is too proud, he had Philippe named instead. Yes, yes! He gave us his hired man as deputy. He wrote *Poil de Carotte* to get back at his mother, who is such a good woman!"

A copy of *Poil de Carotte* is going around Chitry, with an annotation something as follows: "Copy found by chance in a bookstore. It's a book where he speaks ill of his mother to revenge himself on her."

You think about death as long as you hope to escape from it.

My imagination is my memory.

It is the wild apple trees that have the most beautiful flowers.

The bird feels nothing when you clip its wings, but it can no longer fly.

I cannot look at the leaf of a tree without being crushed by the universe.

I am afflicted with prose the way I was once afflicted with verse. When this is over, in what shall I write?

Guitry at the Exposition. In front of the Petit Palais, a bent old woman says to him:

"Would you give me your hand, monsieur, to help me up the stairs?"

"Why, of course, madame!"

And so we see the handsome, elegant Guitry, embarrassed, a bit red in the face, climbing the stairs while holding out his fist, to which the old woman's hand clings like an old hawk. I hear:

"Oh, when you're young . . . There should be a railing."

"Oui, madame."

At the edge of the last step, he frees himself. Then he tells me:

"I am making sure that I still have my watch, because that's the way it always ends."

What is that star? We read its name in a book and think we know it.

There are moments when life goes too far; art must guard against all exaggeration.

The task of the writer is to learn how to write.

Pale, almost white clouds, that, standing out against the blackness, seem like the smoke of the thunderclaps.

At the Exposition from Great Britain, Guitry shows me paintings by, I think, Reynolds. No need to explain myself: it is beauty that reaches to the bottom of the heart. It is painting for lovers. Children, little girls, women, leave us with the sadness of not being loved by them.

JULY

In some Edgar Poe translated by Baudelaire, Guitry selects a complicated passage and reads it to us. Capus, however, has the courage to ask what it means.

[Philippe comes to Paris]. He is even redder in Paris than in the country. He finds the Gare de Lyon real nice.

Philippe writes to his wife for the first time. She will answer, and then he will write again. It surprises him to be calling her Madame on an envelope.

He does not like to stay in the house. He walks around the Rue du Rocher until the soup is cooked.

Guitry tells us this:

Pasteur presents himself at the house of Madame Boucicault, the widow of the owner of the Bon Marché. They hesitate to let him in. "It's an old gentleman," says the maid. "Is it the Pasteur of the dog rabies?" The maid goes to inquire. "Yes," says Pasteur. He comes in. He explains that he is going to found an Institute. Little by little he becomes animated, clear, eloquent. "And that is why I have taken on the duty of bothering charitable persons like yourself. The least contribution—" "Why, of course!" says Mme. Boucicault, as embarrassed as he is. After a few trivial remarks, she takes her checkbook, signs a check and hands it, folded, to Pasteur. "Thank you, madame!" he says. "You are too kind." He glances at the check and bursts into tears. She does too. The check was for a million francs.

Guitry's eyes are red and I have a lump in my throat.

And we talk about goodness, full of a benevolence that melts within us and does us good before, alas! we do any good to others.

Philippe has had tears in his eyes only once in his life: he was watching the hail come down.

AUGUST

One should not speak of rereading the classical masterpieces—one always seems to be reading them for the first time.

The white blackbird exists, but it is so white that it cannot be seen, and the black blackbird is only its shadow.

SEPTEMBER

She is affected; each one of her words seems to have been rolled in flour.

OCTOBER

Every one of our works must be a crisis, almost a revolution.

The best in us is incommunicable.

The tree has never been able to make its shadow circle it completely.

Time passed through the needle's eye of the hours.

NOVEMBER

A dream is only life madly dilated.

Writing. The most difficult part is to take hold of the pen, dip it in the ink, and hold it firm over the paper.

I, I, not an enthusiast? A few notes of music, the sound of flowing water, the wind in the leaves, and my poor heart runs over with tears, with real tears—yes, yes!

I wait, in order to work, that my subject begins to work on me.

DECEMBER

Every moment my pen drops because I tell myself: "What I am writing here is not true."

To be content with little money is also a talent.

Victor Hugo is so great that we don't even notice that he has the ridiculous name of Victor, like you and me.

Chaumot

My father. A while ago, my hand on the doorknob, I hesitated. Out of fear? No. Before opening the door, I gave him time to leave the room to which he must be returning.

One day, I shall surprise him.

The dead, like the air, inhabit—it is certain—the places where we are not.

Tomorrow, my mother will be dead. I shall know another ghost.

There are places and moments in which one is so completely alone that one sees the world entire.

The body is a good dog for our blind soul.

"Ragotte likes to put nails in her wooden shoes," says Philippe, "because they clatter on the church floor when she goes to Mass."

A sky as clean as a glass.

The Philippes come together at their hearth like the cooking pot and the bellows.

At four o'clock in the evening they put the soup on the fire. Their hands stretched out to the flame, they sit musing, while the clock ticks, like the heart of the house.

The clock has more life than they.

1901

We no longer know what love is. The thing itself is lost, drowned in a verbal deluge. It is impossible to come through to reality, which should be simple and clear.

JANUARY

The union of the Philippe couple can be symbolized by their artless habit of eating their soup, all their lives, out of the same bowl.

This Journal empties me. It is not a work of writing. Just as making love every day is not love.

I am alone in wearing my ribbon on my overcoat. The others are braver. At the risk of catching an inflammation of the chest, they boldly open their coat so that the buttonhole of the jacket may be seen.

Victor Hugo. His landslides of verse.

A little girl caged behind a large, undulating harp, scratching with her fingers the bars of her cage.

The poems of our dreams, upon which reason acts, on waking, as the sun acts upon the dew.

FEBRUARY

I tell Tristan that when, at thirty-four, Victor Hugo was traveling incognito, he found his name written on the walls of churches.

"On his second visit," says Tristan.

[Baïe]. After her scarlet fever, her whooping cough, her touch of pleurisy, what will she have? The face of a doctor who no longer knows what to think. That persistent fever—he ends by saying:

"I am not worried, but I should like to see Hutinel." . . .

Marinette and I don't dare look at each other—eyes say too much. How easy to imagine the death of that little thing! That short, rapid breath is her life, Why doesn't it suddenly stop? . . .

Eleven o'clock at night. Still those forty degrees [104 F.] of fever, the burning little body . . . Under her closed lids, is she asleep? . . .

At her bedside, her mother wishes she could give away her own life in drops of suffering. Beside hers, what is the heart of a man of letters?

With the night behind us, I am no longer afraid of what we may learn from this man [Dr. Hutinel], who, although he will speak of things I do not understand, is still prone to error . . . Consultation between him and Collache in my study. It takes a long time . . . Then . . . The tongue, the inside of the eye, the abdomen. Auscultation.

An unintelligible word to Collache. Perhaps it is the only true one.

He straightens out, says a few reassuring words and goes once more into my study with Collache. This is the difficult moment. They come up again.

"Well, madame, here is the truth. No danger for the time being . . ."

A prescription. Nourishment. The chest in a vest of cottonwool. Convalescence: first in the country, then, in summer, a month in Switzerland . . .

"And Rostand's country?"

"No." . . .

"It is I," says Hutinel, "who discovered Rostand's pneumonia."

Baïe. All of a sudden, the fever drops like a burnt cloth.

Hutinel finds her better . . . We tell him she is tired of milk. Immediately, he quotes *Tartuffe*:

"An understanding can be reached with heaven. Give her milk, but disguised . . . Give her chicken, chopped fine in bouillon, cooked fruit . . ."

Glancing every instant at the picture of *Poil de Carotte* above Baïe, he forgets himself, almost goes into a trance.

Their adverbs: bacteriologically.

Baïe anticipates and thinks fearfully of the possibility of her never being well, of spending the rest of her life in bed; but it does not occur to her that she might die. Lying there in her sickbed, she is the only one to have no thought of death.

Like a pot of glue, he always has his hat on crooked.

The sort of anxiety one feels when one writes or speaks ill of God.

To write the life of Poil de Carotte, but without arranging anything: the unvarnished truth. It might become the book of M. Lepic. Put in everything. Oh, how it bothered me when he took me into his confidence concerning that pretty, dirty young girl!

Sometimes, I should like to learn that I am not his son; it would amuse me. Not even to say that I am his son. Say everything with a naked cynicism.

After his death, finish with a sort of hymn in his honor, done in small strokes. A book that would make you want to howl and weep.

I should not be writing for my little sister . . .

Sometimes, he would be telling me his life, sometimes I should be guessing it.

He quotes Christ at every turn. Vacations. Stage-coaches. He carries his bag. His photographs.

I tell this story as a man.

"Mme. Lepic had a certain freshness. I went to bed with her without love, but with pleasure." . . .

Why should I refrain from writing this book? Half of its characters are already dead; the rest will die tomorrow or the day after, and not because of my book.

His first daughter . . . "I used to run up the stairs, to see her a moment sooner."

"And me?"

"You? Oh, you came without my wishing it."

"It doesn't hurt my feelings" . . .

He despises me because I don't seem to be preoccupied with women. His scabrous stories embarrass me more than they do him. I turn away, not to laugh, but because I blush.

The hunt. Jealous scene between him, Maurice, and me. All three of us wanted to beat each other up.

M. Lepic talked very much about his love for that little girl. He may have had as much affection for me, but he talked about it less.

"Since then," he said, "I don't care about anything."

It would amuse me to learn that he was cuckolded, and that I am not his son.

It would explain a great deal, but those things just don't happen to me.

Tristan must be more and more convinced that no one is worthy of tying the laces of his shoes, because they are never tied.

MARCH

Baïe, her face repainted with fresh colors.

Nothing so disgusts one with life as to leaf through a medical dictionary.

To load my sentence well, aim well, and score a bull's eye.

We no longer know what love is. The thing itself is lost, drowned in a verbal deluge. It is impossible to come through to reality, which should be simple and clear.

Love kills intelligence. The brain and the heart act upon each other in the manner of an hour-glass. One fills itself only to empty the other.

Chaumot

Old women gathering dandelions. It is sunny, and they wear a newspaper on their heads, the same one they wore last year.

APRIL

Rostand is admirable in this, that he has a crowd of admirers and never sees anyone.

Whatever kind of literature it may be, it is always more beautiful than life.

MAY

That chimney smoke! If I could lift the roof off the house like the crust off a pie, I should see a woman bent over a kettle, while the man, thoughtful in a dark corner, waits for the soup to be cooked.

Ten o'clock at night. A landscape. The moon all alone in a sky pure as water. Few stars. In the background, the Morvan a barely visible light blue, like the curving line of the sea on the horizon.

A wide path of white mist over the river, from the moon to the château, which is a dark, sleeping mass. The answering calls of birds, of tree-frogs, and the ringing note of the toad.

Poplars like shadows; horses in the fields, also like shadows. A long, black line: a field wall.

It looks as though the moon were coming to the château on a light carpet of mist.

And what is best is that I have taken these notes on my garden wall, by the light of a lantern.

A great shiver of wind passes over the countryside.

Swallows. Eyebrows scattered through the air.

The circumflex accent is the swallow of writing.

While in flight, they pass along their little cries to each other, from beak to beak.

If I were a bird, I would sleep only in the clouds.

Honorine, stupefied with wretchedness. When Marinette gives her a few sous, she no longer thanks her: she lifts her arms in the air and lets them fall back on her apron.

It is hailing. A disaster! But, once the hail has melted, the peasant does not spend time being sorry for himself: he goes back to work.

JUNE

Now that I wear a decoration, I no longer ask to be served separately in restaurants: I am content with the general table.

I wanted to see what, in this little village, could be done with truth alone; the answer is: nothing.

Philippe can't keep from laughing when, after he has done something I ordered him to do, I say "Thank you."

There are Poils de Carottes among the little chicks. I see one that his mother chases out from under her wings, pecks at furiously, perhaps simply because he has a black spot not placed according to her taste.

The cow. Her calf was taken from her this evening, and given to Raymond, who will raise it. What will she do now, this good mother who never tired of licking her sticky offspring, no doubt more for the taste he had than out of maternal feelings?

When she comes back to the stable, I almost expect a scene. She sniffs the straw on which the calf had lain, and lows softly. She eats a little of the straw, which carries the taste of the calf.

But the door to the hayrack opens. Although she comes from the meadow, she avidly eats the hay that Philippe gives her. She is still calling her calf, but she lets Ragotte milk her. We give her bread, which she swallows.

In two more days, she will remember nothing. Her maternal feelings, which seemed so deep, will have vanished.

Marinette. At the cemetery, she sits down and, under the names incised on the stone, inscribes all our names with a finger that leaves no mark.

There is room for them all.

JULY

Mme. Lepic. Perhaps the truest thing I've done, and the best theatre, is the bringing to life of her eyes and her ears.

She will die unchanged.

As soon as I arrive in the garden, she senses it and sends Marguerite to see.

If I come near the house, I hear the creak of the opening window, and know that her eye and her ear are against the crack.

She tries hard to find something to say to me. At last, in that voice of hers, hard, shrill, and dry as a burst of powder, she yells so that the whole village may know that she has spoken to me:

"Jules, Marinette just went out of here. Did you meet her?"

"No!"

That "No!" that escapes from me like a sound of lead, is all I manage to say to my mother who is soon going to die. I walk on. She, with her face against the bars, hurt, powerless, does not draw back at once. She does not close the window yet, so that the neighbors may think that our talk has continued.

How often my father felt like strangling her when she came into his room to take a towel from the closet. Then she would go out, and come back to replace the towel. He sealed the closet.

AUGUST

A walk through the fields. Each one of my steps raises a friendly ghost, who comes with me. The memory of my father, his smock blown out by the wind.

Marinette appears, and the earth is gentler to the feet. She tells me that her father almost named her Solange, after the daughter of George Sand.

God, so much mystery—it is cruel, it is unworthy of you.

Taciturn God, speak to us!

SEPTEMBER

Honorine is in her eighty-seventh year, but she can't tell the age of her brother, who has just died.

Language has its flowerings and its winters. There are styles bare as the skeletons of trees, then comes the flowery style of the full, leafy, bushy school. Then comes the pruning.

Laziness? Yes, but there is such subtle pleasure in living jealously with one's dreams, and not lending them to anyone!

At table, Philippe wipes his mustache with his crust of bread.

The chestnut, that hedgehog among fruits.

The wind that knows how to turn the pages, but does not know how to read.

To dream is to think by moonlight, by the light of an inner moon.

OCTOBER

Old women have nothing but their mournful talk about their dead. Old men have their tobacco, their drink. If they talk, it isn't necessarily about sad things.

Honorine. Sometimes, at night, when she is waiting for the day that takes forever to come, she sits up on her bed and begins to sing.

Toulouse-Lautrec was lying on his bed, dying, when his father, an old eccentric, came to see him and began catching flies. Lautrec said: "Old fool!" and died.

NOVEMBER

[Cécile] Sorel. I don't have to tell you that I am in love with that woman. What a life, my God, what a life! Suppose I were called upon to possess all the women I am in love with!

I love, I love, I certainly love, and I believe myself to be in love with my wife, but, of all the things said by the great lovers: Don Juan, Rodrigue, Ruy Blas, there isn't a word I could say to my wife without laughing.

On the sidewalk, at two o'clock in the morning.
"And what about *Monsieur Vernet* [dramatization of *L'Ecornifleur*]" says Guitry.
"It isn't working out. No, I just don't hit it right."
I describe it, mumbling.
"Listen," he tells me. "Confidence must come from yourself. I can't give you confidence artificially, but it doesn't seem bad to me."
I start again, and, while making a mess of the play, which I don't even remember, I make him feel it.
"But it's exquisite!"
He is already playing it . . . He seems sincere.
I have a happy moment. I tell the incident to Marinette, who sits up in bed and says:
"I knew it! Oh, I'm so glad!"
I work on it in my dreams.
In the morning, all has faded.

What a peculiar notion for an actress to want to be an honest woman! But, madame, virtue would gain nothing from being general. It is a talent, an art, just like dramatic art. Marinette is an honest woman, and that is fine; but I would not in the least appreciate your being like her, any more than I would permit her to surprise me by displaying theatrical talent.

You, an honest woman! What a funny idea! And when your colleague holds you in his arms, kisses your shoulder, your lips, do you think that at that moment I give a thought to your virtue and that I tell myself: "This actress is very talented, and, besides, she is an honest woman"? There are no virtues that need to belong to everyone: there is finery that is becoming only to certain persons. I like virtue in my wife because it becomes her. If I cannot do without virtue, I will not go and marry an actress, because I am well aware that, in that art of being an honest woman, the actress would never be anything but mediocre, even if she were covered with armor from head to toe.

At work, the difficult thing is to light the little lamp of the brain. After that, it burns by itself.

Keep going! Talent is like the soil. The life you observe will never cease producing. Plough your field each year; it will bear fruit each year.

DECEMBER–Chaumot

Old man Joseph is not married to his old woman; they are only "living together". She is useful to him. She walks forty kilometers every day. She goes as far as Saizy to fetch bags of bread. He knows what road she takes and goes to meet her.

A van is, after all, not a house. In winter, he can often be seen walking around his vehicle, his hands in his pockets, in order to take the air.

Maman in her armchair, near the stove. As soon as she sees me, she goes "Oh! Oh! Oh!" She kisses me with insistence. Oh, that flabby cheek that has nothing of a mother's cheek! And, immediately, she begins to talk volubly. When I leave, she goes with me as far as the garden door, so that the neighbors may know that I have been to see her. She says good-bye over and over again. By the time I have reached the cross she is still talking. I don't dare look at her. I am always afraid of her eyes–cold, glittering and vague.

Fantec is getting to be wonderful. Sometimes I love him as though he were my father.

I ought to have a tiny portable table, so that I could go out and work, like a painter, under the open sky.

1902

As long as thinkers cannot tell me what life and death are, I shall not give a good goddamn for their thoughts.

JR finishes *Monsieur Vernet*, a play in two acts. His earlier plays continue to be given in the Paris theaters.

JANUARY

I give a popular lecture on Molière, at Corbigny, on 29th December, 1901. Nervous all day. I am told that, in spite of the rain, people are coming from Chaumot. Touched, I prepare a few words of appreciation, but, through Philippe's fault, I get there three quarters of an hour early. Nobody. I find this funny, and it restores my aplomb. It is always the same story: you must try to think of something else.

I talk an hour and a quarter without fatigue, and I don't touch the glass of water. That ought to make my stock go up! They listen on their feet, without shifting their weight . . .

Poor people! I may have overdone it; it is time to be a saint and cut short . . .

They feel respect only for the person who is "not dumb" . . .

The workman and the peasant come to a lecture in order to be amused or instructed; afterwards, they may pass judgment. The bourgeois comes only for the purpose of passing judgment . . .

The applause is violent and short. The ladies feel that their presence absolves them from further effort.

Of *Prix Martin,* by Labiche. Guitry and Capus remark at the same time; one: "It's a masterpiece!" the other: "It's idiotic."

Louis Paillard [a friend of JR's] comes all warm from Corbigny and brings me news. Philippe told him:

"They can say what they like! Not one of them could have talked for an hour and a quarter without a shot of brandy."

The chaplain of Corbigny, a young man, seeing *Poil de Carotte* on a table, says to the people present:

"Listen! I can vouch for it, that from a literary standpoint this is absolutely worthless."

The curé, a good man, said to Paillard:

"You gave Monsieur Renard a dithyrambic notice" [in the local paper].

"I only wrote what I thought."

"You surprise me. Anyway, be careful. That man is dangerous: the ideas he has on religion!"

"He is sincere."

"Is that possible?" . . .

They think I have political ambitions. They don't dare come too near me, for fear of being tarred by my brush. But they admit that I am an honest man.

Please, God, don't make me die too quickly! I shouldn't mind seeing how I die.

Philippe's dream was to have a big, blue gardener's apron, with a pocket for his clippers. That way, he wouldn't crack his trousers when he kneels down. How were we to guess?

FEBRUARY

The theatre is the place where I am the most bored, and where I most enjoy being bored. Guitry can't get me out of his dressing room.

Snow. All France is dead.

I have a horror of rhyme, especially in prose.

A beautiful line of verse has twelve feet, and two wings.

A dream. In a dormitory. I in one bed, she in the next one. I tell her: "Come over!" She comes. I begin by pressing her against me, and feel her under her chemise. Then I dare bring my hand down, bring it up everywhere, over the soft skin, the hard breasts, and I cover her face with kisses. As, for an instant, I detach my lips from her, I see, at the foot of the bed, the study master looking at us, stern, distressed. She hurries back to her bed. I hide under the sheets. It is over.

This morning, I wake into a light gratitude, shivering like a tree that has spent the night steeped in moonlight.

So long as thinkers cannot tell me what life and death are, I shall not give a good goddamn for their thoughts.

I have lived on all the planets: life is a joke on none.

Weep! But not one of your tears must reach the tip of your pen and mix itself with your ink.

The curtain of memory draws back only when it wills.

MARCH

The unexplored expanses, always fallow, in the best friendships.

Chaumot

The peasant has two weapons: his vote and his greeting.

When he notices that you have the weakness of caring about his hellos, he can make you very unhappy.

APRIL

Dreams swift as a pigeon passing in front of a window.

Style. When "amethyst" comes along, "topaz" is not far behind.

Music. I owe some of my most pleasant day-dreams to the hum of a tea kettle.

When Ragotte eats, she always looks as though she were doing something holy.

The odor of a great house: the acrid odor of servants who never wash.

At the zoo. The kangaroo jumps in precise and rubbery leaps the whole length of his alley, and, with his two front paws against his chest, seems to be saying: "I'm terribly sorry, but I can't help myself; when the mood seizes me, I must do this."

The parrot's beak, black as the bottom of an old purse with a leather tongue.

Spring. As though we were to begin lunch with a few sprigs of lilac, and end it with a bowl of apple blossoms.

Sarah's attitudes: she can look intelligent when she is listening to things she does not understand.

MAY

First communion: the little boys are all wounded in the left arm.

With men like Chateaubriand and Lamartine you travel in the air, but without direction.

"I once served under an adjutant," says Guitry, "who one day gave us as a point of direction 'the center of the fog.'"

Truth is not always art; art is not always truth; but truth and art have points of contact, which I am seeking.

Father, I am forgetting you! My poor old papa, you are finished.

Ragotte looks like a little monster carved out of wood.

The security of a new shoe-lace.

JUNE

Yesterday morning, I did not like Shakespeare. Last night, the last act of *The Merchant of Venice* moved a pound of my heart. I was rubbing the corners of my eyes with my fingers. Am I to be compelled to like Shakespeare?

You may write as few books as you like: people persist in not knowing them all.

I shall end by not being able to do without Paris. I shall acquire an anxiety in solitude. After a day, not of work, but of study, a walk on the boulevards in the evening–those lights, those women, those people–takes the shape of a reward.

A dream neither produces nor warms. It is something dead, moving in space without freedom, like the moon.

I keep for my little village all that I have not given to the great city of Paris.

With the help of my lantern, I have found a man—myself. I shall keep him.

When I think of all the books still left for me to read, I am certain of further happiness.

The writer must create his own language, and not use that of his neighbor. He must be able to watch it grow.

JULY

It's many a day since I've felt ashamed of my vanity, or even tried to correct it. Of all my faults, it is the one that amuses me most.

Reverie is nothing but thought thinking of nothing.

AUGUST

Chitry. It's the first time, but I should prefer anonymity. A while ago, as I passed in front of the inn, I heard men talking loudly, and one of them almost shouted, while still restraining himself: "Poil de Carotte!" Shall I, some day, have to turn around and answer: "And you, what do they call you? Poil de bum, or skunk?" Is Poil de Carotte going to make this country uninhabitable for me?

To think that, if ever I get to be eighty and am compelled to be a "strong-arm" mayor, the urchins will run after me, calling me Poil de Carotte.

The partridge makes a noise like a blade being sharpened.

Bouquin's dog barks every evening, not at the moon—there isn't any—but at mystery. He renders his homage to God.

I know the exact point at which literature loses its footing and no longer is in touch with life.

My father asking for the hand of Marinette on my behalf.

He did put on black gloves. He talks about everything, listens to Marinette play the piano, says: "Yes, enough," and gets to his feet.

"And the request, papa?" I ask, worried.

He smiles and says nothing. You guess that he is thinking: "Wouldn't it be rather ridiculous to start hunting for the suitable words? The fact that I am here, for the last quarter-hour, in your sitting room, talking to you, doesn't it prove, madame, that I am asking your daughter's hand for my son? Isn't it sufficient?"

And Mme. Morneau, who has prepared a dignified reply, waits.

"We can consider the request made," I say. "Can't we, madame?"

"Why, yes! Why, yes!" says she, confused, and laughing too.

Whereupon we all laugh, and kiss one another.

Prose is the language of happiness. Since we're married, dearest, I haven't written a single line of verse, alas!

Not the smallest charm of truth is that it scandalizes.

SEPTEMBER

Honorine, her jaws deformed by hard bread.

A cloud, for Philippe, is a threat of rain. He does not know that certain clouds have no function but to be beautiful.

At four o'clock, they eat bread and hard cheese. They drink white wine, but Ragotte drinks only water, because wine drops into her legs and breaks her arms. What havoc!

Philippe does not like to dream: it tires him as much as to do the harvest.

Marinette. The Philippe couple call her "our lady."

When Myrrha is taken hunting she is so happy that she immediately starts picking up and bringing in whatever she finds: a leaf, a piece of wood. In spite of the partridge bones I give her at the table, she likes Philippe best. He is more to her taste, and my distinction is lost on her. She refuses to give me the partridge she retrieves. If I try to take it from her, she holds on harder, and the entrails come out.

Words must be nothing but the clothing, carefully made to measure, of thought.

OCTOBER

Return to Paris. I say to Capus:
    "Well, confound it, my sentences are more difficult than yours."
    "Yes," he replies. "Take one word out of your sentence and it crumbles. Take everything out of mine and it's still there."

Suddenly I stop in the middle of a field, and this question alights on me like a great black bird: "By whom were we created and why?"

NOVEMBER

Guitry watching *Le Pain de Ménage*. I feel like telling him: "What are you smiling at? Because it's not good? Perhaps you expect too much."
    There are moments when the deepest friendship does not hold by a hair. You say to yourself: "Suppose I went away? Are we about to embrace, or to bite each other?" Everything hinges on a smile, on the sound of the first thing said, on a gesture.

Guitry. It is a pleasure for him, at Paillard's, for instance, to ask me which I prefer, Chablis or Graves, and to observe my anguish in front of the waiters who stand watching me, smiling, pencil in hand.

DECEMBER

Winter sun, clear and weightless—rather acid.

1903

You say I am an atheist, because we do not search for God in the same manner: or rather, you believe you have found Him. I congratulate you. I am still searching for Him. I shall search for Him ten, twenty years, if He lends me life.

JANUARY

An old woman, all rumpled by time.

In my church, there is no vaulting between me and the sky.

Supper at the Ritz to celebrate the hundredth performance of *La Châtelaine* by Capus . . .

[Jeanne] Granier, laughing too much, quotes one of my childhood sayings to Sarah Bernhardt, who pretends not to have heard.

I say to [Eve] Lavallière, in something of a shot in the dark:

"Your face is pleasing by its openness. I would guess that you have high moral qualities."

And the poor little woman, all of a flutter, takes my hand over and over again:

"Oh, I am so happy! Of all Guitry's friends, you were the only one who seemed to despise me, and it made me miserable. I thought you would never like me, and now you tell me this! Oh, I'm so happy!" . . .

Say to one of them [actresses]: "You're pretty," and they just don't care.

Say: "You have talent," and it means a little more.

Say: "You have moral qualities," and you discover that each one is a little girl at heart.

Guitry tells a story well. He is not afraid. When he lies, it is not his nose that quivers: it is mine.

MARCH

When you rejoice over being young, and notice how well you feel, that is age.

To have dinner once or twice a year at the house of a rich friend, to drive out once or twice in the depth of his carriage, to admire his paintings, his luxury, that is all that is necessary for a decent man to feel himself rich.

Irony is an element of happiness.

Monsieur Vernet. Yesterday, at Maire's [a restaurant], I read to Antoine, [Jeanne] Cheirel, Signoret. I read before lunch. After the first act, I feel it has carried so well that, sure of myself, I go on to the second. (The reading has not moved me.)

The second act read, and, to my mind, badly read, I look at Antoine. He looks at me a long moment, then:

"Are you satisfied with your second act?"

"Yes."

"Entirely satisfied?"

"Entirely satisfied. You're not?"

"There is something . . ." says Antoine.

It is as though my whole play had crashed to the ground.

"But what?"

"After M. Vernet's scene, you lost me. There's a hole."

"And I didn't get you back?"

"No, I wasn't following any more."

"Well what should I do?"

"That isn't my job, but yours. For an act and a half you held me; then you no longer held me; that's all I know."

I question Signoret and Cheirel. Signoret admits that as a matter of fact there was a slack spot after the scene of the declaration. They add that it is nothing, but with Antoine I feel something more alarming, as though he had not understood.

Monsieur Vernet. Reading of the second act by the actors. First, a certain hesitation, then, in the scene between M. Vernet and Henri, I feel, in spite of the stumblings, that it has clicked.

Antoine, who is sitting next to me, turns toward me, which I coyly affect not to notice. I hear:

"You've got it!"

"Yes, don't you think?"

"That was all it needed. There will be a hundred performances, on the same program as the play by Lorde. Remember what I tell you."

Signoret tells me: "At the first reading, I had not seen your big scene in its proper perspective. Now I see that it's by far the best."

I go home with a heartful of success.

They're amusing, those readings by actors. The public should be let in on them. Corrections, things left out by the copyist. From time to time, an actor who has nothing to say escapes behind his manuscript: the author fears a yawn.

Tasteless cakes that make you appreciate bread.

The sudden naturalness of an actor when, during a rehearsal, he interrupts himself to speak to the prompter.

APRIL

Dumas Fils had a great deal of talent for his period. Since then, we have learned a new language. Perhaps all that is necessary is to rewrite all that, I don't say with more talent, but with different words. In twenty years, perhaps the same thing should be done with the plays of Capus and Hervieu.

They say that the Théâtre Libre is malicious. But how boorish Dumas is! He treats women with the contempt of a freed slave.

L'Aiglon. Yes, it's another world, but, every moment, it moves me. Rostand forbids himself nothing, and he profits by this. He uses all the strings, but he ties down all the birds with them, eagles as well as goldfinches.

You may be full of horror for war: Victor Hugo and Rostand almost succeed in making you accept the butcheries of Napoleon.

All this crushes me. And all that movement makes me want to write plays with people *sitting down*.

Monsieur Vernet. Antoine is not there . . . Signoret, very worried over comparisons that may be made with the book, would like me to change the names. I reply that this would be an unnecessary little piece of cowardice.

Cheirel no longer knows where she is . . . I told her to be a little melancholy, but Antoine, who feels that melancholy is not good theatre, tells her to be "good-natured."

I insist; I take my two acts to Antoine, and, while he is getting himself out of his Napoleonic rig, I read the scene as I had read it to Guitry, to Brandès, and achieve the same effect. He says:

"Yes, that's it! You've got it! If it were played as you read it, the effect would be certain."

At Guitry's, Noblet tells me:

"Since I've been in the theatre, this is the first time that an author has that simple, excellent idea of reading his play once more to the actors after a certain number of rehearsals."

MAY

Dress rehearsal of the second act.

Preoccupied with their clothes and the last adjustments, they all act badly, besides trying to do it the way I want them to and against Antoine, who, furious, no longer knows a word of his part.

"It's a marvel!" Wolff tells him.

"It has pull," replies Antoine, "and Renard will ruin the whole thing by making us play it like that."

He says to Alfred Natanson:

"It's impossible to give him what he wants."

To me:

"It's filthy. Taking it like that, the whole play gets away from us."

"I don't care!" I say. "I'd rather have a flop with my play acted according to its proper sense, than a success without me."

"All right! All right! I'll play it like that. Oh, don't worry! I won't deceive you, but, some evening, I'll play it the way I want it, in front of the public, and then, you'll see!"

Didn't sleep, last night. Shivers, burnings, fever . . .

Marinette, admirable, full of courage, will send Fantec home to tell me how the first act went over: "Very good," "Good," "Went over," "Did not go over."

"Don't worry!" she tells me. "I swear I'll tell the truth. I'll even stay below rather than go above it."

. . . Gradually, I calm down. Apart from the question of money, what is all that theatre madness?

Ten o'clock . . . Fantec comes to fetch me. The entire first act is a success.

I arrive in time to hear the applause for Antoine in the scene of the second act.

He comes out and tells me:

"A bit of drag in my scene, but an enormous effect. Smashing success."

Blum, Tristan, other friends come: it is very much like *Poil de Carotte*. Cheirel, enchanted, kisses me. We all embrace.

"No hard feelings," says Antoine . . .

I have supper with Guitry and Brandès. Go to bed gay, unconcerned.

The next morning I open the papers. Mendès icy, the *Echo de Paris* silent . . . a press that has no connection with the success of the opening night. Stupefaction. Depression. In that case—what? . . .

The press has stopped the sale of tickets.

"Oh, the swine!" says Antoine . . .

Not a request to publish, to translate. Nothing! It's a financial disaster. But I stiffen. If I had a subject ready for three acts, I would start on it right there.

At the opening, a gentleman:

"It is the first time that I fail to be bored by a declaration of love on the stage!"

A woman, at the scene between the two men:

"Is that good!"

And the arguments with Antoine begin again.

"I have only one regret," he says: "Not to have shut myself up alone with my actors, and locked you out."

"No!" I say, "I swear you would not have locked me out of my own play!"

"Don't take on your mean look. The misfortune about this play," he adds, "is that it was rehearsed in two theatres at the same time."

"You mean that I went to Guitry for advice? What do you take me for?"

Any moment, we might be about to devour each other. I tell him:

"That scene must be played on a bench, like the one in *Poil de Carotte*; and you play it too unfeelingly."

"What you ask for is not theatre."

"I know it: it is human. Try it all the same."

And it ends up with: "Your play is exquisite," and a box-office of 3500 francs, one of the best four Saturdays of the year. And everything ends up with money. And Antoine admits that it is *Monsieur Vernet* that is making money.

Franc-Nohain:

"You will never make much money in the theatre. I thought you might, after *Poil de Carotte*, but—"

Tristan:

"You will make money in the theatre. After *Poil de Carotte*, I didn't think you would, but—"

The wind that makes the chimney look as though it were smoking while on the run.

A sentence must be so clear that it pleases at once, and that it is reread for the pleasure it gives.

An author should not go too often to see his own play: he would notice that the mediocre parts are those that go over best, and he would tend to be mediocre in his next play.

JULY–Chaumot

The ignorance of the peasant consists of what he does not know and what he thinks he knows.

The women are a little ashamed of their curé, who makes them angry with his coarseness; but they are afraid of him. That curé might well be the devil. They're not sure any longer, and, poor distracted souls, go back to him.

Cousin Nanette to her daughter:
"Aren't you ashamed to dress up like that? Do you think you're not a peasant girl any more? Don't you dare call me mother!"
And she kisses her, full of pride.

Maupassant does not observe: he imagines reality. It is all approximation.

Nature is never ugly. How well the trees breathe!

The somber green of a wood when a cloud passes over it.

Mown meadows, still green; grazed meadows, already yellow.

As I was reading poetry, a quail called. Ah, poor peasants who do not know such emotions, you deserve all human pity!

The water quivers: it looks like a lake of silver leaves.

Patina of time on the roofs. You no longer see the tiles, but a curtain of white and yellow moss, soft to the eye.

Mme. Lepic. The busy actress, hardly knowing any longer what she is doing, what she is saying; having one remaining thought and purpose in life: to be on the stage every minute of the time.
She goes and rents a room some place, convinced that if her house were free her children would at once become friends again.
She says that she tips Philippe fifty francs; also, that she must have a bottle of brandy in the house at all times—not for herself, of course! So now Philippe will no longer accept a glass of wine from

her, and drinks water when he works in the garden. Vexed by these refusals, she makes out that there is less than nothing in that garden, while it costs her a fortune.

Philippe, who used to believe she was kind, understands at last the life my father led. He adds, speaking to Marinette: "I refuse her glass of wine or her shot of brandy, but you understand, madame, that I would never refuse yours."

She plays at being a well-organized woman. She needs a little wood. She has the wherewithal to buy it. What would people say if she didn't leave, in some corner or other, enough to have herself buried?

She still keeps giving away things. At first it was out of charity, then it was out of pride. Now it is out of humility, to be tolerated, because she is afraid of being left alone.

When I pass by her door, I hear her voice, high-pitched and metallic, without inflections. She is talking all by herself, in order to make me believe—for she has seen me, she was on the lookout for me—that she has visitors, that she is not neglected.

And she plays the lady: she wears ruffles on her sleeves, which enrages Cousin Nanette.

Philippe. Fresh air and garlic will make him live a hundred years.

Not a breath of air, and the leaves and branches stir as though moved by the tree itself.

Happy people have no right to be optimists: it is an insult to sorrow.

When you see Ragotte, with her enormous breasts, standing by her son, tall, wide, and fat, you feel like saying tenderly: "You are a good cow, and you have produced a good calf." She gave to her children all the thick life of her breasts.

Without her bonnet, she looks a hundred years older.

Who has not seen God has not seen anything.

AUGUST

The compass. That little blue needle seeking the north is a lesson to our incredulity.

If rest is not to some extent work, it quickly becomes boredom.

When she was taking her cow to the meadow this morning, Ragotte heard screams, screams! She ran to see, and found, in a field, a little lad keeping Bouquin's sheep. He was yelling out of lonesomeness, because he has been hired out to Bouquin as a little shepherd, since St. John's day. He is twelve years old. He was homesick for his parents, who live in Mouron, and he started yelling again, and big tears ran down to his chin.

Maman. She weeps because Cousin Nanette said to her: "He does not love you! He does not love you!"

"Oh!" says she to Marinette, "You don't know how a mother suffers!"

A butterfly got on the train at Clamecy and traveled with me.

SEPTEMBER

Delicate mountains, barely rippled by the wind.

There are first-class funerals, as though we went to heaven by rail.

Mme. Lepic weeps over the death of the countess.

"She was ill for a long time, but she passed on without suffering, and she died (fresh burst of sobs) in the arms of her son."

Yes, yes! I see you coming, maman, with your little family scene.

You can go through all the shops in Corbigny without finding a fingernail file or a toothbrush, and the only sponges are for washing carriages.

There is nothing as meanly practical as religion.

You say I am an atheist, because we do not search for God in the same manner: or, rather, you believe you have found Him. I congratulate you. I am still searching for Him. I shall search for Him ten, twenty years, if He lends me life. I am afraid I shall not find Him: but I shall still look for Him, if He exists. He may be appreciative of my efforts.

Yesterday, on the way back from hunting, Philippe said to me:

"The other day, Joseph (his youngest son) had a queer face on him."

"Oh?"

"Yes, when he saw that when Mme. Renard paid him his wages, she didn't give him a raise. It is true his cousins, for instance, get more than him."

"If Joseph feels that he doesn't earn enough, there's just one thing for him to do: leave."

"Oh, I didn't say that because—"

"You were wrong to say it, Philippe, especially now that I have a whole family of servants on my back. What you said is not going to help you. Mme. Renard will not be pleased! It's a fine reward I'm bringing her!"

She told me:

"The face on you! I thought there had been a hunting accident."

I call in Philippe and Joseph. Managing not to fly off the handle, I tell Philippe that he has hurt me, that I have lost confidence in him, that he has placed a wall between us, and, as for Joseph, that he can look for a job.

They are struck dumb, eat only a spoonful of soup, don't sleep at night, and, the next morning, Ragotte is crying.

"Oh," she says, "I told them: 'Don't talk about that!' and Paul said like me, and Philippe too, and he was wrong to talk. You will pass over it, madame, you are so kind!"

I feel like casting La Gloriette overboard, but the tears of this poor woman—out of pity, also out of selfishness (always, always!) I soften: we have never seen Ragotte cry but once before.

"We've never been so mortified," she says.

All day, Philippe has shelled peas, sheepish and dejected.

An old, white-haired servant, cast down because he has said something foolish, not knowing how to go about making up for it, what can be sweeter to our miserable vanity of masters!

"I have no religion," says Borneau, "but I respect the religion of others. Religion is sacred."

Why this privilege, this immunity? . . . A believer creates God in his own image; if he is ugly, his God will be morally ugly. Why should moral ugliness be respectable?

The beauties of literature. I lose a cow. I write about her death, and this brings me in enough to buy another cow.

I can see Chitry. I cannot see Chaumot, of which I am part. Is it above that thatch that my bust will stand? It seems to me that my eyes of stone will see this landscape, so well composed.

Last night, long talk with Philippe, on the bench. He wasn't eating any more, he was so convinced I was angry.

He tells me that, after my reproaches, Joseph began to cry on the stairs, and hung on his neck repeating: "I don't want to leave them! I don't want to leave this place!"

I talk, I talk, and, to everything I say, Philippe answers:

"Oh, I know, I know! Never was I so sorry I talked."

Concerning Marinette, he says:

"I never saw her put out before, and there are many times I do things wrong and she says nothing."

In the darkness, our voices grow softer. At one moment, it seems to me that he is wiping his eyes. If I don't embrace him, I should like at least to clasp the hand of this man whose hair is white as my father's was.

When we stand up, he says:

"It's a long time since my heart was so light."

"For me," I say, "there are no servants. We are all brothers."

These words, I feel, surprise him, but do not penetrate.

Ragotte was very ill, last winter, for the first time in her life. She doesn't know what she had. She doctored herself by drinking two liters of hot water. She couldn't get up. She was hot all over, except in the back, which she couldn't have kept warm "even by putting a house on it." She was coughing, coughing! At last, she vomited blood: it didn't frighten her. In fact, it was the only thing that made her feel better.

Philippe, who was sick too, could do nothing. But one evening, Paul, after looking at her, said:

"I'm going to make you a broth."

He went over to Bouquin's and bought an old hen. He quickly plucked and cleaned it, and he made a potful of bouillon. It was uneatable. It was foul, says Ragotte herself, but she drank it all so as not to hurt Paul.

Ragotte has big, delicate feelings.

Her ideal: to pay what you owe and owe nothing more.

Ragotte is probably the last peasant.

OCTOBER

Bucolics. The great day of their lives: they played cards from one o'clock in the afternoon until six o'clock in the morning, and, by way of taking a rest, farted like gods.

Curé Bongard, as he was reading his breviary on the road, heard cries: "Caw! Caw!" He accused the children of the gardener of the château. But they were real crows: they confessed everything!

Ragotte loves sweet stuff, the most tasteless cakes, like a little girl. This addiction has come upon her since she is old.

Marinette promised to bring her a stick of barley sugar from Corbigny. Ragotte couldn't believe it, and she sucks it, blushing, as though she were coming home from school.

The falling leaves tumble away on the ground what life is left to them. One of them has the honor of being pursued by my kitten.

Literature does not have the power of creating emotion out of something that contains none.

Days filled with harshness: the sun does nothing but hide itself. Suddenly, in the distance, a village breaks out into full light.

Yes, I always give to beggars. They walk more than a kilometer to come and say good-day; it is well worth two sous.

Oh, the feet of the beggar seen below the door, while the dogs are barking!

Maman. When the impression she makes on me is least disagreeable, she strikes me as a child.

Marinette says to her: "Why don't you come to La Gloriette; you could say good-bye to Jules."

At first she doesn't understand.

"Yes, to La Gloriette! To my house!" repeats Marinette.

Maman, speechless with joy, recovers her twenty-year-old legs. She comes, sits down, looks around, admires everything.

"Is that all this cost you? Impossible! It can't be!"

At the end of her visit, Marinette calls me. I kiss and give my hand. It goes off quickly and well. No one is there.

She leaves, happy and voluble. But, once she is in the court, she hears Mme. Thibaudat coming through her garden. Immediately, back she comes and says:

"Good-day, Madame Thibaudat!"

And adds: "Good-bye, Julot!"

Julot is me. She wants to show that she is on the best of terms with me, with her son, with Julot, and that she calls me by nicknames.

Poor mother!

The glory of finding myself in little reading books used in primary schools.

A grasshopper played the fiddle; a tree-frog, the bag-pipe.

DECEMBER–Paris

One can quickly discover if a poet has talent. In the case of prose writers, it takes a little longer.

The People's Theatre, what nonsense! Call it the Aristocrats' Theatre and the people will come.

Maman made the trip with a soldier who came from Nice; she introduced him to Marinette, at the station.

I had prepared: "Hello, maman. Are you feeling well? Had a good trip? Make yourself comfortable." I was only able to say hello and give her two kisses with lips dry and pressed together.

In her "Oh! this Paris!" there was something warm, intimate, that was never given to Poil de Carotte.

Maman had said to the soldier: "At the station, when you see a young and pretty woman, that will be my daughter-in-law."

"He was charming to me, this young man," she said, as she presented him. "These are my dear daughter and my grandson, who is fifteen."

And the soldier saluted, smiled—a little too much, for he had a missing tooth.

Maman was not getting off the train: nobody had shouted: "Paris!"

She is a child. She can never have suffered much.

She says: "I had a turkey, but it was dead, while that lady had two live geese that cackled." She adds: "One ran away."

"I am very happy when I am traveling: I never have to go to the toilet."

On her cheek, an old-age pimple, which she keeps picking.

She coughs all the time, not because she needs to, but to let us know she is there.

She is quite fond of Marinette, but at bottom is a little piqued because Marinette is not afraid of her.

It amazes me that when I was twelve I didn't lead her by the nose.

She hasn't seen Paris since '70. After barely the time to see it again by gaslight, from the Gare de Lyon to the rue du Rocher, she says: "My Paris hasn't changed."

She has her charm, a sort of charm I am impervious to.

She is still the same. The doorbell rings. She disappears, but she wants to see. You think she is far away, and all at once the door opens. "Oh! you're here?"

She admits: "I didn't know how to take or keep my place with your father."

Maman is afraid of dying suddenly. She would like neither to be ill long nor to die too quickly. She wants to have the time to say what she has to say.

She will still be talking!

1904

*How quickly one could lose one's head! Any moment, there is
nothing between us and death but the paper hoop of the clown.
It should not be too difficult to jump through!
We would not reappear, that is all.*

JR's plays are published in book form.

JANUARY—Paris

Maman can chatter for hours with a little girl, with a cat: its purring
is enough in the way of response.

What would suit her, would be a kitchen giving on the stairs, so
she could open the door and see who is going up.

She is one of those old women who think they are clean because
they wash the tip of their nose every day.

She doesn't lie: she invents. She invents everything with meaningless facility, even to her dreams.

One can't say that she steals: she moves things. She takes a thimble she knows someone is hunting for. She doesn't give it up immediately: she lets you hunt.

These are not the thefts of a grown-up person: they are the little thefts of a magpie.

Maman says it is she who introduced shoeblacking in Chitry. Before that, people blacked their shoes with soot from the bottom of the cooking pot.

"There is your photograph on the wall," we say to maman.

"Fine thing you've hung there!" says she.

"I'm like old people," she tells us. "I no longer have any appetite."

And she swallows a bowlful of coffee-with-milk, and, of us all, is the only one to eat her entire roll. She notices this:

"This isn't appetite: it's greediness."

She says she doesn't sleep any more. This morning, she gets up at nine.

"I didn't sleep all night," she says. "I dozed off this morning. I didn't hear any sound"—she sleeps close to the interior staircase—"and, there, look: my watch was stopped."

She says: "My daughter," but, speaking of Maurice and me, "these gentlemen."

She remembers insignificant details from the past, but has forgotten that she lost her first little girl. My father wanted to kill himself.

If she doesn't happen to think of the word "cemetery," she does not remember that her "dear departed" are resting there.

Her jealousy of Marinette's contentment, her rage against this woman who manages to be happy with a man whom everyone considers unbearable.

Maman is about to go away furious because Marinette is happy.
She says to her:

"No wonder you're happy, with the kind of disposition you
have!" and she begins to cry.

She writes to the people of Chitry that she has been very well
received, but that she is not feeling well and is coming home. She is
getting ready to say that we didn't want to let her go.

She hears us talking in Baïe's room. She opens the door, appears on
the threshold like Lady Macbeth, says: "Poor little Baïe! Dear little
chick!" and closes the door.

"If someone comes into my study, she sits on the stairs to listen.

"What are you doing there, maman?"

"I am keeping warm."

"You're in a draft. Come in here: you'll be more comfortable."

We hear her weeping in bed.

"It was a good week I had, but it's all over!"

We are about to feel sorry for her, but we notice that only her
mouth is crying.

"I'll go upstairs to say good-bye to Jules."

"Don't bother," says Marinette, "he's coming down."

At the foot of the stairs:

"Good-bye, my Jules, and thank you. Good-bye!"

She presses my hand, kisses me on the left temple, through her
veil. She really does have the tremor of tears. I haven't said a word.
It may be the last time that she kisses me—and that I fail to kiss
her.

My mother!

In the cab that takes her away she says bitterly:

"Such visits only leave you sad."

"Why, maman!"

"I mean, my dear, they leave a big emptiness."

[Philippe comes to Paris]. His get-up: One of my overcoats, an old hat of Maurice's, a pair of Fantec's shoes. He came as he was, bringing only a shirt

His insistence upon walking behind Marinette.

"Are you tired?"

"No."

"Do your shoes hurt?"

"Oh, no!"

After swallowing a big plateful of soup, he went out, but only for a turn around our block, for fear of getting lost.

What surprises him most is the gas, the water that comes up into the kitchens, the vegetables at Potin's, the new potatoes in January.

I have all my mother's faults, neutralized.

The Doll's House. What a lot of meaningless things made to sound profound! Nora's attack of liberty probably just deserves a good spanking. In this play, things are turned upside down as quickly as they are straightened out elsewhere. A business of forgery that ends in a discussion. The only man is this bank employee who wants to hang on to his little job. All that, however, in spite of its being lengthy, badly constructed, and arbitrary, is not boring. It is a change from our everlasting adultery.

The role of Nora throws light on the talent of (Mlle.) Desprès. It shows up its good points and its limitations. Gifted and stubborn, this young actress prefers this part to all others because she will never be able to play it well.

Soeur Ernestine [later to be called *La Bigote*]. I believe I have found an ending for the play; I carry it to Marinette like a bowl of warm milk, and I see by her eyes that I was not mistaken. I hurry to Guitry's. As soon as I say, "I have it" his joy bursts forth, he does not know what it is, but he wants to play it this season.

In the most complete friendship there is always a little empty space, like the space in an egg.

Joy isn't a very pleasant sensation. You are past feeling. It is as though your heart were all whipped cream.

Chaumot

The centipede has—I counted them—only twenty feet.

MARCH

Perched on the edge of his chimney, the sparrow day-dreams like a little chimney-sweep with his job done.

Philippe, always a little weighted down with secrets: he carries the moon in his apron.

Honorine lets herself be eaten alive by vermin. The other day maman washed her hands and face.

She would like to have for herself the bacon we give to her daughter-in-law for her soup. When her daughter-in-law—her granddaughter-in-law, rather—says: "Grandma, your soup's ready," she answers: "I don't want none of your soup," and with her foot makes the motion of upsetting it. Then, she eats it.

Since she is dirty, her granddaughter-in-law made her take off her petticoat with the intention of washing it. The old woman, in a rage, threw the petticoat into the fire and burnt it up.

Like all old women, maman is afraid of death. They don't know that death is beautiful: they truly believe the devil is approaching.

APRIL

A village like Chaumot or Chitry is the best proof that the world makes no sense.

Honorine has practically become earth.

She is dying every moment.

She ties her forty sous in her handkerchief. She will forget it, but she will not lose it. She has long ago given up blowing her nose!

Elections. It is an ugly moment. You hardly dare take a step, say good-morning, shake a hand. You seem to be begging a vote. A smile looks like an entreaty.

The voter believes himself to be the master. There's a confusion there. Why, no, my good man! You must vote in order to do right by yourself, not by me. It is I who am doing you a favor.

The curé tells them fairy tales and promises them the moon in Paradise.

All the mayor cares about is his sash.

Who among them will take a close look at the peasant and tell him: "You've been asleep for centuries. Wake up!"

Mme. Cahouet, former schoolmistress, talks with the murmurous assiduity of a country priest.

"Oh, those articles of yours! I don't hold with their ideas, but I admire their vigor, their acuteness."

At last, a woman who talks to me about my articles!

A poor beggar, an "old-soldier" type, has written the word "Dunce" on his hat, in chalk. He thinks this is a stroke of genius, that will make his fortune.

Maman. When all is said and done, a woman who at one time was young, and was called Rosa by the ladies of the region.

Branches in tears.

Paris

Rain. Little ten-sou pieces of pure water, thrown by the clouds into the canal.

MAY

The schoolmaster of Héry waylays Chaumot people in the woods and tells them they will never find another one like me. He describes what I am. He has bought one of my books.

They would love and approve of what I say, if I said it in songs.

Marinette finds she is past understanding. She says I look illuminated. She weeps.

"It seems to me," she says "that you are no longer a writer."

"I am the same as always, only developed, broadened."

The little flame I should like to see in her eyes still does not appear.

"So much effort for such small results!" she goes on. "Those people who don't understand you, who think they are better than you are, it is grotesque!"

"Nothing is lost. If I awaken a single brain, that will be enough. Besides, one shouldn't think about results."

"You are risking so much!"

"What do I risk? Insults, perhaps a duel . . . But if I didn't do what I must do, I'd die of boredom, of disgust."

"Yes, yes, you talk like an apostle. You will end up a saint."

"Why not?"

"A lay saint."

"If that is my destiny . . . My intelligence flows clear as a brook, and will never stop."

Cherry trees. Armbands of flowers on all the branches.

The curé passes in front of Marinette, haughty, enormous. Under his biretta, long grey hair like a horse's mane. Cassock lifted by his belly. Poor Paul, who is with him, would like to raise his hat to her. He hangs back a little, but so does the curé. Paul's hand gets as high as his stomach. With a terrible look, the curé halts its progress.

A sprig of lilies-of-the-valley is delightful; a wheelbarrowful repels.

The beggars know me. They lift their hats to me and inquire about my family.

One must keep an eye on the peasant. He still sniffs with joy the odor of the nobleman, the powerful, the rich.

Maman says: "The most beautiful day of my life: the 15th of May, 1904, when my son was elected mayor of Chitry."

Elections. I may have been the only one who took them seriously.

Honorine has a joint missing on one finger. She no longer remembers whether she lost it while harvesting, by a stroke of the sickle, or through an infection. She only remembers that the pain made her want to throw herself into the river.

As mayor, I am supposed to look after the maintenance of the rural roads; as a poet, I like them better neglected.

When you talk with a peasant, you realize that you know nothing; or it is as if you knew nothing, because you can tell him nothing.

JUNE

A style as pure as water is clear from, as it were, wearing itself down on stones.

Maman is turning into a little girl again. She likes to be scolded, and she wails with the voice of a child who hardly knows how to talk.

The wireless, yes. But I wonder where our graceful swallows will perch?

Branch of a cherry tree, as voluptuous as the arm of a woman.

Five little lads from school. They play in the dust.

In their shoulder bags, the first one carries bread and hard cheese for himself and his brother; another, again for himself and his brother, has bread and an egg in a little tin pot; the fifth, the oldest, has a piece of brioche, left over from a comrade's first communion, and cherries. All drink well water.

The father of the family enjoys the liberty of letting his children starve. Almost all the peasants drink wine, almost all eat stew at noon; the child eats hard cheese.

JULY

In Brittany [with Guitry] 23 to 27 June.

Brest. The old wooden boats that seem to float on the very surface of the water.

The broom, brilliant flower of this dark soil. Gold set in coal. Facile contrast, sure effect. Not very clever! "But you had to think of it," God would say.

Nothing so sets you up as having an unknown lift his hat to you on the road.

. . . And here is the armchair of Sarah Bernhardt; this is where she sat. It had been nameless. Now, all the English carry away a piece of it.

I was about to do the same: but I am not an Englishman.

AUGUST

The bird's nest, that graceful witness to its trust in us.

Maman talking about "sin"!

"I had my faults, I still have my faults, but I've always had the right to walk with my head held high."

Yes, but papa cuckolded might have been happier.

I present my book to a schoolteacher.

"What do I owe you?" he asks.

Toward morning, when you can't sleep, you are possessed with genius. You see luminous things on that black canvas. In the dark, you scribble on a piece of paper.

The next day, all you find is meaningless scratches.

Shooting stars. Shots of light, without sound or smoke. It is the opening of the hunt in the starry fields.

Kindness is not natural: it is the stony fruit of reason. To do the slightest kindness, you have to seize yourself by the skin of your behind and propel yourself forward.

Maman. A great actress to whom life gave nothing but poor parts. Bent over in the garden, she catches sight of us and remains bent while she rehearses her lamentations.

An old woman tries to place a bundle of hay on her shoulder with her pitchfork. She can't do it. She calls Philippe.

"You will kill yourself!" he says.

She answers: "So much the better!"

Philippe lets it pass; and she does not press her point. He places the pitchfork for her.

"Wait till I catch my breath," she says, weakening.

She puts her handkerchief between her shoulder and the handle of the pitchfork. She can no longer be seen. The hay has taken the place of the old woman and moves away.

From their burrows, the rabbits watch the passage, O Shakespeare! of this walking alfalfa.

Even the desire to kill seems to have left me.

A quail, its wings spread over its half-dozen young.

An old hunter from Héry calls our attention to a quail in order to keep us from noticing a hare.

The starling perches on the nose of an ox and feasts on ticks.

Philippe trembles when he points out a hare in its burrow. I am too close. A little farther over. There.

The morning of the opening of the hunt. The moon was on our left. I loaded my rifle by its light. The sun rose, drinking up the moon's vapor bath.

It was sensuous, that way she had of pushing a drawer shut with her behind.

SEPTEMBER

The lark rises. It comes to rest on a lump of earth a little farther on.

It is dangerous to carry a gun. You think it doesn't kill. I shoot, not in order to kill the lark, but to see what will happen. I come near. It is lying on its belly; its claws flutter, its beak opens and closes, yawns open: the tiny scissors are cutting blood.

Lark, may you become the subtlest of my thoughts and the dearest of my regrets!

It died for the others.

I have torn up my permit and hung my rifle on a nail.

Idyll. Philippe has torn his trousers: his thigh shows. What white skin he has, this old peasant with dirty feet!

A woman in the grass:

"You wouldn't have a pin?" he asks.

"A pin. What for?"

"Look!"

She laughs. She puts in two safety pins, one at the top of the tear, one at the bottom.

"There," she says, a little flushed.

Philippe, his leg taut and stretched, looks like a great hunter.

I listen at doors, even at keyholes, for the sound that life makes.

They say:

"You can do what you like, madame. There are heads that breed lice. I can clean her head all I like with snuff; nothing helps. She still has lice and pimples."

"Cut off her hair."

"That beautiful hair?!"

And my mother says:

"Oh, yes! there are louse-heads. And there was never one like Jules's."

The cry of the screech-owl passes over the house. Marinette wakes up and, thinking that Baïe is calling, asks:

"What is it?"

The only reply of the owl is a faster beating of its wings. It is something, at least: more than God has ever said.

The slow jaws of the peasant. When he eats, he appears to be thinking.

A peasant. There is a simple man. Examine him, take your time, and, after two weeks, three weeks, ten years, write a page about him: in all you say there will probably be not one word of truth.

Each note I put down must have the flavor of a strawberry.

Asnan. They have a wonderful knoll, pink with heather. Their Virgin, attached to her pedestal by iron clamps, blesses them and turns her back on the people of Grenois.

Oh, to live eight days in this village of Grenois, which is there in its entirety, like a seashell, and climb the mountain each evening! God loves heights.

204 ❋ THE JOURNAL OF JULES RENARD

A peasant from Asnan:

"Monsieur, I'll tell you the why-for. I don't know the why-for, but I'll tell you: the vine doesn't pay any more. Everyone makes wine for his thirst, but we don't sell, and if we could sell we wouldn't. Used to be that the wine merchants came. They don't come any more: it's too easy to travel. They go and buy their wine far away, where it's cheaper."

If God forgives me, I'll ask him to let me relive a life at Grenois.

Villages less known than the stars.

Honorine no longer uses sheets: she sleeps all dressed on her bed.

She tried to climb on a chair in order to wind up her old clock. It doesn't do her any good, because she is deaf, and she can't lift her head to see the time, but she likes to watch the pendulum "dingling". It keeps her company.

Marinette winds the clock for her and says:

"What time?"

"Make it six o'clock."

"But it isn't even four!"

"Never mind! Make it six o'clock anyway. It makes no difference: it rings."

When you ask them to take certain precautions for the sake of public health, they say you are making trouble.

A fine for whoever will think up a thought about life. Leave life alone!

We have perhaps died already three or four times.

All the walks one can take on foot around one's village: that is one's native land.

A dream. A woman is scratching around on my head. I say to her:
"Write to your husband: 'Sir, a great wind is blowing. I have
killed four lice.'"

Invisible beings burst out laughing.

Stars: fireworks that have stayed in the air.

This being kind all the time is killing me. Of what good can I be if
I deny myself any little meanness?

Truth. Some novelists do get her out of the well, but then they
promptly wrap her in blankets.

Since the day that I got to know the peasant, any bucolic writing,
even my own, has seemed a lie.

From far off, the wood is nothing but shadow; close to, nothing but
night.

Advice to hunters: to go out some time without their gun and walk
through the fields where they have killed. The magpie becomes
familiar. The partridges sit still until one comes quite near. The
prunelles wait to be picked, and the juicy little wild pear.
    The ox stops and looks around, and the ox that follows him licks
his hindquarters with a lazy tongue.
    The meadow draws to itself the entire green blanket.
    And one has not murdered: that at least is something.

The spiders have done their science studies, with particular emphasis on geometry.

OCTOBER

Walk. The partridges no longer fear me. I should like to be a partridge. What a pleasant time they seemed to be having there, in the field, behind the hedge!

Team: two oxen, four wheels connected by a wooden shaft and two cross-beams. Seated behind his oxen, the man sings. A primitive; a king of the earth going home to his village.

Two screech-owls, believing themselves to be alone, call to each other from two oak-trees.

Two old women sit at the edge of a field to mind their geese; unless their geese are minding them.

The wood is dressed in colors, as though in Sunday clothes.

The fields are wonderful, green and soft to the eye, well laid out in length and breadth.

Yes, yes! They are ignorant, hypocritical, spiteful, but they are in illness and want. Empty your pockets, instead of giving advice!

A tree drops a leaf on my shoulder and goes back to dreaming.

I write little, but I have so long to live!

The return to the city. Oh, it is cowardly to go where there are lights, to leave this poor little village when it is about to turn so cold and dismal!

But they like winter. They say:

"There is nothing to do. You can rest. You stay long in bed. You don't sleep all the time, but you're comfortable."

The icy water in which, all night, the washerwomen have the impression that they have left their fingers.

First frost. A little ice on a cabbage leaf.

One day I believe in human progress, I call for it with all my might; the remaining six days, I rest.

Nature and the peasant. All that physical and moral wretchedness under our sky! And the earth is covered with villages.

An ox gazes at me. He looks kind, and gentle, and patient, like Fantec. Marinette would have kissed him.

I walk well in wooden shoes in the stubbled fields. Having made my fortune in Paris, I learn, in the country, to walk in wooden shoes.

Socialists, you and I can no longer agree. You want to become richer, I am trying to become poorer. You will get there before I do.

I no longer dare to say: "Tomorrow I shall work."

Evening. The moon, Jupiter. Moving mists. A troop of trees fording a river. A dog out hunting. Invisible oxen.

The château is dark; but a light in the dining-room shows that people are dining there in accordance with the rules of etiquette.

Slender poplars, heavy elms. As the mist moves, some are drowned while others raise their heads.

You hear the stream running in the very depth of the earth.

Now and then everything is drowned. It is a deluge.

Your mouth filled with dampness, you go home. You are a little scared.

Everyone believes his little domestic happenings to be extraordinary. A most peculiar thing.

In the theatre, the aim is to create this little illusion for all.

Yesterday, Paris seemed to me a sad, dirty, beastly city, not in the least deserving the expense to live in it. I never saw such crowds in the streets: is the metro turning them away?

[After an evening at the theatre.] The public is as critical and as for-bearing as ever; with the same incoherence.

Mme. de Noailles did not find to her taste my article in *Le Matin*, in which I replied to Vauxcelles's examination of literature. She is the goddess. I was lacking in respect. I wounded the goddess in her talent.

She has too much genius and not enough talent: talent is genius amended. She has the kind of genius peculiar to talented people who lack taste.

Ah, what beautiful things we should write if we were without taste! But voilà—taste is French literature entire.

At the *Salon d'Automne*. Works by Carrière, Renoir, Cézanne, Lau-trec.

Carrière is good, but a little too clever.

Majesty in vice—that is Lautrec.

Cézanne, barbarous. Many daubs of renown would have to be admired before one could admire that carpenter of color.

Renoir is perhaps the best of all and, at last! one who is not afraid of painting: he puts an entire garden on a straw hat; and at first you are dazzled. You look more closely, and the mouths of the little girls begin to smile, and with what subtlety! . . . and those eyes that open like flowers! They make mine open too.

Vallotton. The meaningless dreariness of a paper hanger.

The beautiful life of Cezanne, entirely spent in a village in the South (Midi). He did not even come to his autumn exposition. He would dearly like to have the ribbon of the Legion of Honor.

That is what they all want, these poor old painters whose life was admirably spent, and who, near death, watch the art dealers getting rich on their works.

Renoir, old and wearing his ribbon, says:

"Yes, yes, say what you like. You let your head hang, and then your eye catches that bit of red, and, I swear, you raise your head again!"

Vollard, the art dealer, says:

"I hold it against my father that he taught me nothing about art. I can't talk to a pretty woman on the street without feeling like a vulgarian."

Guitry lies, but why should I care? I don't look for truth in him, I have it in myself.

His journey through Italy: unbelievable towns, Vesuvius spewing jets of fire that fall back on his face, Venice: all those houses growing out of the water, it doesn't make sense!

"But how can you go there and not stay?"

"You must do as I do," he says, "come back to Paris for your bread!"

"And get mud on your face again . . ."

"I'll have to do that too."

It is mainly from memory that I take notes. When I look, when I listen, it never occurs to me that in a moment I shall have to write.

NOVEMBER

Lazy like all sedentary men who have too much time in which to do their work.

The plume of the house is its smoke.

The window pane has faults that double the stars.

Chitry

At the mairie. Wedding. I almost address the bride as "Madame" when asking her to sit down. I make a speech. The ladies weep. Signatures: neither the father nor the mother can sign their name. The bride lifts her veil. I kiss her and, thanks to Philippe who warned me, I give her twenty francs for her firstborn.

Objects. Something has vanished. We hunt for it in vain. Suddenly, it is found.

"That was where it was!"

"Hm!"

"Since you found it, it must have been there."

"I'm not so sure."

Winter. A pale smoke in the diffused pallor of cold air.

DECEMBER

This woman had loved so much that when you drew close to her you could hear, in the delicate shell of her ear, the far-off rumor of love.

Reality has killed my imagination, that used to be a fine, rich lady. The other one is so poor that I shall have to go out seeking my bread.

Ah, yes! to be a socialist and make a lot of money.

How quickly one could lose one's head! Any moment, there is nothing between us and death but the paper hoop of the clown. It should not be too difficult to jump through! We would not reappear, that is all.

When I am not thinking about myself, I am thinking of nobody.

I am not, I have never been, and I can never be anything but a poor artist at 200 francs a month.

[Get-together of the socialists of Nevers.]

. . . There are songs. Children make a racket. The waiter passes, collecting ten-sou pieces. They will not allow me to pay: I am a guest. I look like a stranger, with my little red ribbon and my modest mien of a man who believes himself well-known.

1905

In order to work, you clear away the obligations in your life.
No visits, no meals on the outside, no fencing or promenades.
You will be able to work, do fine things—and, on that wide gray
sheet that is a day, your mind projects nothing.

JANUARY–Chitry

The restless but clear-sighted—hence active and healthy—mind of a man not engaged in work.

[The peasants]. Their mania for concealing the fact that they are ill. Their ignorance in regard to illness. Outside of "My back hurts, I can't sleep or eat," they know nothing.

The entire countryside trembles with cold.

Paris

Coolus relates that d'Annunzio, the first time he called on Sarah Bernhardt, stopped a few paces from her and said, like one inspired:

"Beautiful! Magnificent! D'Annunzian!"
After which he said:
"Bonjour, madame."

The simple life. We need a servant to close the shutters, light a lamp, as though a decent man shouldn't find pleasure in these little household chores.

The moments when, I know not why, I feel like punishing myself.

To be a socialist with your reason costs nothing, but let emotion enter into it and you are ruined. The reasoned socialist may have all the defects of the rich man: the emotional socialist must have all the virtues of the poor one.

Slavs: people who write between the lines instead of on them.

I am very fond of looking at the faces of young women. It amuses me to try to guess what they will be like when they are old.

Does a flame give out its brilliance in order to cook a pot of soup?

I have an anti-clerical mind and the heart of a monk.

Rapid as the thought of a zebra.

The cat asleep, well buttoned into its fur.

Certainly there are good and bad times, but our mood changes more often than our fortune.

FEBRUARY

Walk with Marinette. An old man with his valet, the latter dressed like a gentleman and walking next to and even a little ahead of him.

That sudden impression of being in a dream. What is this town? These people walking around? All the confidence that habitually sustains you and allows you to live is gone.

It is a spring-like hour.

There are some poor people who care about Paris as though it were a village.

Visit to Chaumot

Nature is of a fineness! It looks like a sketch of itself.

Cold, damp sheets. You go to bed in your sweater, underpants, heavy socks, dressing gown, and shiver all night.

The river steams with the cold.
   The villages, no longer smothered in their leaves, seem to say: "At last! We can breathe!"
   Immobility, deep sleep of nature: the cock's crow goes straight up.

Days when it seems as though the world would like to die.

MARCH

Henri de Régnier tells me that Mallarmé could not understand how anyone could write the words "God" and "heart." "God," in a sentence, creates the effect of a stone in a spider's web. "Heart" no doubt evokes too material an image.

I live like an old man. I read the papers a little, a few pieces out of books, I set down a few notes, I keep warm, and, often, I nap.

I am no longer capable of dying young.

In the taste of life, there is something of a fine liqueur.

Little Joseph, Philippe's young son, died last night. There was another one who didn't give a damn about immortality!

The sparrows say of us: "They build houses so that we can build our nests in their walls."

Yes, what death does is interesting, but it repeats itself too much.

Any writer who is polite, who acknowledges a letter or the receipt of a book, does not believe himself to be famous.

Work is a little like a prison: how many pleasant, passing things it keeps us from seeing!

A day lost in dreaming about work put off from hour to hour. Notes, a good find or two, perhaps; the trimmings, not the essential.

I envy Marinette: she has cooked our soup.

I have done nothing. If only I had driven a few nails, split some wood, sowed carrot seeds, written, on no matter what subject, a few lines that would be published tomorrow and for which I would receive a few sous! I should not have done nothing, I should not have wasted my day.

In order to work, you clear away the obligations in your life. No visits, no meals on the outside, no fencing or promenades. You will now be able to work, do fine things—and, on that wide gray sheet that is a day, your mind projects nothing.

I suddenly abolished a number of things I was very fond of: poetry, fencing, fishing, hunting, swimming. When will I abolish prose, literature? When, life?

Nights without sleep, long nights in which the brain lights up like a big city. What a beautiful procession of dreams that you believe to be alive! By morning they are no more. The awakening, that pitiless sweeper, has pushed everything into the sewer.

[After an interview given to a reporter]. I told him that peasants often marry for love, and he prints the exact opposite.

Spring. The smoke that comes out of the roofs is the color of periwinkles.

[At the zoo]. In the midst of these exotic birds, the barnyard hens look like good, honest housewives.

At the slightest ray of sunlight, an eagle hides in a dark corner of his cage.

Always afraid of life, I can't take my eyes off it once it has passed by.

Duse in *La Femme de Claude*, a play in which Dumas was particularly artificial.

I had expected a suffering melancholy, subtlety: instead, vigor, a little on the order of Guitry's. Gestures with the arms, the hands. A more powerful Réjane, minus the tricks, and, to my surprise, many theatrical attitudes.

It bothers me, that Duse should like this coarse role of *femme fatale*. Is she more an actress than a woman?

She plants a resounding kiss on the lips of the man she wants as a lover. Our actresses have made something fairly repellent of the long, silent kiss, the end of which one awaits with a certain revulsion.

Duse in *La Dame aux Camélias*. In the darkness of the theatre, some get fidgety, others sleep.

This woman is truly a harmony. The entire first act is a caress. She has a way of exercising her seduction on cushions and of hiding her head under a pillow! . . .

She is not pleased. She finds the public cold, the box-office receipts insufficient, the curtain calls too few.

APRIL

Duse. Beauty, nobility, intelligence. Her face never "freezes." In the Goldoni play she has a witty face: she does not make her face play at wit.

When she leaves the stage, she goes out: she does not tear herself away.

Chaumot

Nature is not so much green as the color of vert-de-gris. The leaves of the horse-chestnut are uncurling.

On the road, Honorine stops often, surprised to find herself still walking.

Maman says to me:

"How awful you look! Here are your Easter eggs."

If she were not prevented–but she will be prevented–she would come to La Gloriette every day. When she is left one day without news, she is almost in tears with worry.

She always says the wrong thing: to those who believe themselves ill that they look fine; to those who are worrying about their health, that they look poorly.

I shall never get used to that woman, I shall never get accustomed to my mother.

She brings me a dozen Easter eggs, and impresses upon Marinette that nobody else must have any, not the maid, not Philippe, not even Fantec and Baïe. She wants me to eat them all. Twelve hard-boiled eggs: she wants me to suffocate.

Man should be considered from the point of view of the naturalist, not the romantic psychologist. Man is barely a reasoning animal.

Maman no longer says, "My son," but "Monsieur le maire." Pretty soon, she will say *vous* to me, like a curé's mother.

She says:

"My daughter-in-law has wonderful taste! and her husband lets her do whatever she likes. He has complete confidence in her. She deserves it. I'll not be here to see it, but you will see how beautifully they will fix up my house! It will be something marvelous."

I understand the tree: it does not reason.

If Fantec should fail in his exams for his baccalaureate [in France obtained at the end of high school studies], maman will say: "He was too smart: he went beyond them!"

A little hate cleanses us of kindness.

MAY

When maman returns in a carriage with Marinette, she casts a defiant look in my direction.

How difficult it is to be kind! I hope I shall never succeed.

On Sunday evenings Philippe is bored. He replaces the strap on a wooden shoe and goes to plant potatoes. He walks the dogs and weeps for little Joseph.

Maupassant. He was too often satisfied with verisimilitude.

Every morning, oxen sprout in the fields like mushrooms.

Sometimes maman will drop her needle and stare at Marinette:

"My poor girl, suppose you were to take sick! At night, I wake up and think out loud: 'If only nothing happens to us!'"

Style. I always stop at the brink of what will not be true.

The rich man's hardness of heart is not a serious defect in the eyes of the peasant.

The train, the automobile of the poor. All it lacks is to be able to go everywhere.

God is no solution. It doesn't arrange anything. It makes nothing right.

Perhaps, if you were to become too perfect morally, you would become like that little stunted tree I see through my window, that no longer produces a single leaf.

Maupassant. A man who is never caught short. He teaches nothing, and the nature of his feelings does not earn him our affection. Good morning, good-night. There can be no intimacy with him.

Maman asks, as though it were an honor, to be allowed to darn my old socks.

The breath of a book one opens! Oh, how that one stinks at the mouth!

I take joyous little excursions in my interior, on my lake of ennui.

Dreams. When reason takes a walk, madmen dance in one's brain.

JUNE

It seems to me that my love of nature is making it more beautiful: grass seems greener than it used to be, and the tiles on the roofs more pink.

Marinette is afraid that I shall lose interest in life. I tell her that vulgar ambition must not be confused with joy of living.

"With you," she says, "everything comes out right. I am not afraid of the bull. With one motion, you shoo him away from us."

"Marinette," I tell her, "I used to be afraid of death, and today I can smile when I imagine myself lying in my coffin. I used to be afraid of storms: I no longer give them a thought. I still fear the pain of a sword's thrust, but not of being killed in a duel. The essential thing is that I not lose you; and as for the rest! . . . I have given up everything that a Hervieu may be looking for; I have not given up the main thing. I used to be afraid of certain ideas: I am no longer afraid of any. I admit of everything, except causing a person one loves to suffer; or simply causing suffering. You have prevented me from becoming a satiric poet. I keep within me a fund of essential naïveté that is like eternal youth. I defy anything that is beautiful, alive, and simple not to affect me."

The sparrow: a delightful little bird that does not sing.

Pity, yes, yes; but what you don't mention is their dirt.

A sky of the blue of a peasant's blouse.

The one who loves and admires us most is, after all, the one who knows us least.

Hay carts like moving hayricks.

I remember that special odor that I smelled at the time of my father's death. It comes back to me every year, at the same season. I shall end by believing that it is the taste of death.

I discover it is the smell of roses that have faded in their vase.

My father died in June, the season of roses.

Work is a treasure; I know it by counter-proof.

To what good are mementoes, even photographs? It is comforting that things die, as well as men.

The pleasure of working only on Sunday.

Such a soft evening! Of whom could I ask forgiveness?

Without its bitterness, life would not be bearable.

JULY

On Laziness! Ah! That is one book I shall have to write! The fool who understands his foolishness may no longer be quite such a fool, but the lazy man can be aware of his laziness, bemoan it, and remain lazy.

If you fear solitude, do not try to be just.

Maman exclaims:
   "Ten meters of fabric! Oh, my dear, it is too much, a thousand times too much! Nine meters would have been quite enough."
   Like a little girl, she wants to show Marinette a hem she has stitched, so she can be told she has done it right.

For miles around, I am called in for the distribution of school prizes. I have a reputation, like a bone setter.

Medusa was poverty.

The lower classes do not constitute the public.
   I warn you that the lower classes sweat, smoke, spit, pick their nose, pare their nails with a knife. Out of tact, you will say nothing, but will you have the stomach to stay?

The affecting life of a tree, that throws itself desperately about as if trying to take a step.

The working man goes to political meetings, the bourgeois to lectures.

Ragotte will never ask a thing from the two children she has left. They do not look like the two who are dead: she doesn't know where they came from. The other two were exactly like their father and mother, but not these.

The joy of a finished work spoils the work you are about to begin: you now believe that it is easy.

The beautiful page written by a tree endures only a season.

AUGUST

Socialism must come down from the brain and reach the heart.

Mougneau. His joy in digging up something—an old iron, a tool that wasn't burned in the fire—out of the ashes of his house. He never knew such pleasures when he was living in it.

That animal, the railroad train, has appeared in our countryside.

Ragotte docs not know how to wash in a tub. She goes on a hike when she has a rag to wash, in order to do it in the river, in the running water.

　To go to Mass and wash in the river—two holy and ancient customs.

SEPTEMBER

They do not say "to write," but "to mark." "I marked that for him in my letter." It is much more exact.

The pig. All that filth on a pink background.

The donkey with its automobile's voice.

The scorn of a cat for the calf that pursues it in a meadow.

Guitry calls La Gloriette: "Your acre of roof tiles."

Too fast, the auto. So many pretty landscapes where one does not stop.

OCTOBER

The peasant is perhaps the only man who does not like the country and never looks at it.

Maman is sorrowful; with a sincere sorrow that, though it will not last, is affecting.

She is beginning to believe that visits do not take care of everything.

A sad picture: an old woman, on a chair balanced on two legs, bending toward a fire of two smoking logs. Behind her, the cold of the kitchen.

She finds in her son the same silent man that her husband was; what's more, the husband remains invisible.

To wait on her, she has Lucie, a little maid in mourning, who never seems to be there.

She is losing the strength that made her talkative. Her words drop into the fire, and others do not follow. There are long silences.

She weeps and says:

"Oh, I have a lot of grief! Don't you see how much grief I have?"

It may be over her failure to make herself loved as a wife and a mother, over her failure in life.

If only she could disappear, gently consumed and mingled with the ashes on the hearth!

And the wind! All the winds of heaven moan at her door.

I live in laziness as in a prison.

Old age does not exist. At least, we do not suffer from continuous old age at the end of our lives; like trees, we have, every year, our attack of age. We lose our leaves, our temper, our taste for life; then they come back.

We do not have a childhood, a maturity, an old age: several times during our lives we have our seasons, but their course is not well known: it is not clearly laid out.

Philosophy is taking shots blind: you never see where God passes, or if you catch Him or not.

Sheep minded by a youngster so small that the wolf might well eat him when they are not looking.

Autumn. A heavy blanket of fog draws away toward the South, and the North appears, sunny, clear, and cold.

It is enough to have a taste of glory: no need to stuff yourself with it.

Autumn. The sun is so low that already there are corners that do not unfreeze.

Yes, you are intelligent, you understand everything, and you will have the time to understand everything, because you are never stopped by any ecstasy; ecstasy is known only to the artist.

In winter, in the mist of the river, the washerwomen are almost Ondines.

A little before sundown: the moment when my thoughts are so fine-spun that my brain is like a tree stripped of its leaves.

In the middle of the night Honorine goes knocking on the door of a neighbor:

"I am frozen. Warm me up."

The other opens the door and asks her where she comes from. Honorine does not reply. She is put to bed, and it is found that she no longer has a chemise.

Maman. Solitude, broodings by a meager fire while behind her the wind blows through the cracks in the door.

She has one amusement left: to find fault with her maid, whom she sends out to work by the day for all the neighbors. Every time she has fastened on a defect in the girl, she never fails to add:

"Now, I am exactly the opposite. You are young, vain, and dirty. I am old, I am, thank God! no longer vain, and I am clean. You are hard-hearted. Yesterday, you put away all your father's things, his tools, his blouses, his jackets, his trowel, without so much as a tear in your eye. Me, I can't keep from crying just to think that you had that to do. At table, you have no manners, you help yourself before me. I would never had dared help myself before my family."

Maman would not care to be reunited with her loved ones in their unconsecrated free-thinkers' graves.

"Oh, for me, the common grave! That will be quite good enough!"

"Don't talk nonsense," replies Marinette. "You know very well you will have your plot."

But her secret, unconfessed hope is that her plot may by chance be next to that of the countess.

I do not care about the immortality of my name any more than for that of my soul.

If I could arrange it with God, I would ask him to turn me into a tree, a tree that, from the height of the Croisettes, would look toward my village. Yes, I should prefer that to a statue.

Paths must be swept through the leaves, as through snow.

NOVEMBER

Washerwomen like geese that flap their wings on the banks of the river before they enter the water.

A clean-swept landscape in which the fields have kept as little grass as possible, in which the trees have no more leaves to deceive us with than have the houses.

Life is badly arranged. The poor and the ignorant should be rich, and the intelligent man, poor.

Return to Paris. I come to look for work, to hire myself out.

Dejection. If I did not love Marinette, I'd leave by the ten o'clock train. Weakness in Marinette:

"Back there we are kings," she says. "Here, the concierges are as well lodged as we are."

The dining-room seems small. I find the house badly built. The floor creaks under my feet. It is sinister, and it is idiotic: to have, back there, comfort, fresh air, a happy life, and come to lodge for six months in this furnished hotel!

I resent Paris. I have remained four days without wanting to look at it.

Paris: mud, and always the same things. The books have barely changed their titles.

To recover from three days' work, I need three months of reverie.

The Minister of War has resigned: war has been suppressed.

There are days when I imagine myself to be the first who has seen life.

Of my moods, the snow is the one I like the best.

A work must be born and grow like a tree. There are not, in the air, invisible lines along which the branches will set themselves: the tree comes entire from the germ that contained it, and develops free, in the open air. It is the gardener who traces plans, marks paths to follow, who spoils it.

To tell the truth: how the success of *Poil de Carotte* made me believe that I was a man of the theatre, who had merely stopped for three or four hours, as it were; and how difficult it was to start back toward my forgotten village.

Le Mariage de Figaro: a pure masterpiece, light as the air of all time.

DECEMBER

I don't write too badly, because I never take any risks.

You think he is with or without talent according to whether you are on good terms with him or not. Everything is personal like or dislike.

Paris is becoming fantastic. Those buses without horses . . . You seem to be living in the land of shades. And this thought comes back to me: "Aren't we all dead without knowing it?" In these sounds, reflections, in this mist, you walk in anxiety, less with the fear of being run over than with the fear of no longer being alive. The impression of being in an immense cave, and your head in a pulp from the noise.

All kinds of smoke: the blue, light smoke, the white, the gray, the heavy black, all go up to the azure and are lost, and the azure remains.

There are no leaves left; the wind blows only to make a fuss.

Year's end. Our last energy falls away like last leaves.

1906

If I were to begin life again, I should want it as it was.
I would only open my eyes a little more. I did not see properly,
and I did not see everything in that little universe in
which I was feeling my way.

Production of *L' Invité*, one-act play by JR. Fantec begins his medical studies.

JANUARY–Chaumot

The curé has sent around a circular asking who wants religion preserved. Those who were for it were treated to a boiled dinner by the count.

The dripping countryside. Raindrops threaded on narrow branches. Now and then, in a sweep of light, the sun slowly wipes dry a field, a village, a wood.

A cold in the head is much harder to bear than an idea.

Paris

Read *L'Echange* by Claudel. I understand it quite well, and it gives me no pleasure.

Clouds pass across the moon like spiders across the ceiling.

The topmost, thinnest branches of the tree, whose ends seem about to dissolve into air.

Demolder always looks like a mannikin blown up for a trip to the moon. He drinks three liters of wine a day, without counting the beer and all the rest. For a while, his tongue was paralyzed. His anguish at not being able to talk back to his wife. A thousand roses in his garden.

The clock marching, with its heavy, rhythmic tread–One, two! One, two!–while standing still.

Posterity! Why should people be less stupid tomorrow than they are today?

The word that is most true, most exact, most filled with sense, is the word "nothing."

I can believe anything, but the justice of this world does not give me a very reassuring idea of the justice of the next. I am very much afraid that God will go on blundering: he will receive the wicked in Paradise and hurl the good into Hell.

A cat, who sleeps twenty hours out of twenty-four, is perhaps God's most successful creation.

Yes, God exists, but He knows no more about it than we do.

Ah! the divine smile! That He truly has!

It is left to us to repair His injustice. We are more than gods.

I do not know whether He exists, but it would be better, for His own credit, that He did not.

Today, at last, I look at Paris.

Twenty years ago I did not see it. I had only my ambition. I only read books.

Now I stop in front of the Louvre, in front of a church, at a street corner, and I say: "What wonders!"

What was I thinking about until my eyes were opened?

I am going to like everything about you: your monuments, the pink clouds of your setting suns, the cocks and hens on your quays.

I was once a student. I went to register for courses, but tonight, for the first time, I take pleasure in walking through the Latin quarter.

Perhaps genius is to talent what instinct is to reason.

FEBRUARY

In the shadow of a famous man there is always a woman who suffers.

Chaumot

Nature has snow in her ears.

To write for the theatre one must have a passion for untruth.

The green waters of memory, into which everything falls. They must be stirred up. Things rise to the surface.

A tree bandaged in snow, like a wounded finger.

Imagine how man would marvel if he were to see, today, his first rose! He would not know what extraordinary name to give it.

232 of JULES RENARD

Honorine. Death seems to say: ""She has never been sick. It isn't easy to get her. I don't know where to catch hold of her!"

The leaf, poor relation of the flower.

To the socialists: "Yes, let's share! But let's also share loyalty, courtesy, wit!"

The wisdom of the peasant is ignorance that does not dare to express itself.

Forty-two years old. What have I achieved? Almost nothing, and already I am no longer achieving anything at all.

I have less talent, money, health, fewer readers, fewer friends, but I have more resignation.

Death appears to me as a wide lake that I am approaching and of which I am beginning to see the outlines.

Am I a better man? Not much. I have not the energy to do wrong.

Out of forty-two years, I have spent eighteen with Marinette. I have become incapable of hurting her, but am I capable of any effort to do her good?

I regret the time when Fantec and Baïe were so small and so funny. What are they going to do? Am I as concerned with this as I should be?

I think sometimes of my father, very seldom of Maurice, and both have been dead a long time. And my mother still lives. How will I manage to pass from her life to her death while being aware of it?

To get up in the morning, to work, to pay attention to others, tires me.

I still do certain good things pretty well: sleeping, eating, daydreaming.

I also envy people, and run them down.

It does not seem to me that I am better in argument: I shout as loudly as ever, though less often.

On the whole, I don't care about women. Now and then, a romantic dream or so.

I no longer, or hardly ever, read new books. I only enjoy re-reading.

And where do I stand in that matter of fame? Since I shall never have it, I succeed without too much effort in scorning it. I am almost sincere in this, but I say it too often.

There is nothing I desire ardently: I'd have to struggle too hard to get it. Am I neurasthenic? No. That is a serious illness: you suffer and are miserable. My own malady is gentle and full of charm. It seems that the energy I used to have was superfluous. I get along nicely without it.

I have certain feelings of guilt, but am dexterous enough to find fault with myself for having them, and so I diminish them. Truly, I find none of them unbearable.

I used to be afraid of acting when it was dangerous. Nowadays, I am afraid of action itself, or, rather, I have acquired a taste for inaction.

I am still happy when I see my name in print, but I would not give a smile to the prince of critics in order to get it there, unless he came to see me. Yes, yes, in that I maintain a certain style, and it costs me nothing.

The invisible greyhounds of the wind.

A neurasthenic: a man in good health who has a mortal illness.

My literary fiddling around. I go from book to book. I get excited by idea after idea. I stop a few minutes in front of a project, and pass on.

MARCH

Night: day turning blind.

Marinette has never refused me but one thing: the right to dream in the twilight. Merciless, she asks:
  "Shall I light the light?"
  I dare not say no, and she brings in the inimical lamp, which puts all my dreams to rout.

To write neither for the people nor for the élite: for myself.

Your page on autumn must give as much pleasure as a walk through fallen leaves.

Make a summary of my notes year by year in order to show what I was. Say: "I liked, I read this, I saw that." On the whole, no progress.

Imagine life without death. Every day, you would try to kill yourself out of despair.

I reread my notes. Whatever I would have done, my life could not have been much more complicated. What I could have produced more, good and bad, would not have added much to the sum of my works. My works!
  If I were to begin life again, I should want it as it was. I would only open my eyes a little more. I did not see properly, and I did not see everything in that little universe in which I was feeling my way.
  But if I were to try to work again regularly, every day, like a student of rhetoric who wants to be the first in class; not in order to make money, not to be famous, but in order to leave something, a little book, a page, a few sentences? Because I am not at peace.

What causes us to redden with greatest shame under our graying or vanished hair is the vileness of certain desires we had, the very remembrance of which turns us sick.

Do not count too much on society to make reforms. Reform yourself!

Then, you say, we shall all be little saints?

Don't be afraid of that! I give you the rough outline of a vague, unrealizable program. You will always be what you are, only a little less so. One can mitigate one's defects; one cannot extirpate them; but the little progress you will have achieved will illumine your life. You will live with a light heart.

L'Arlésienne, opera by Bizet. Lovely music. How alike all lovely music is! And all those violin-bows growing like the fingernails of a Chinese princess!

A play is good when you are interested in it in spite of its dialogue. It is perfect when the characters say the things you expect them to.

Truth on earth is to falsehood what a pin's head is to the earth.

Pallor: the shadow of shadow.

God will often say to us: "You are not in heaven for fun!"

APRIL

Artistes Indépendents. It is the one place in the world where I am bored the most. After pointillism, building-blockism; and a few young masters who take enormous pains to make us vomit. It is as dull as books of verse or prose published at the authors' expense. In this salon, one is not admitted: anyone can enter here.

Maman. No, no. I am not going to lie about it. To the end, I shall say that I don't care.

She arrives at the house. Marinette has her come in and says: "It's grandmother."

She kisses me (I can't kiss back), and sits down at once, without waiting to be asked. I said: "Good-morning, maman. You're all right?" Not a syllable more.

She doesn't need more. She talks of her own accord. She says:

"I just saw Honorine for the last time. She is going. She doesn't know you any more. She must have a very high fever. Her grand-daughters were giving her something to drink out of a cup that was filthy! but filthy! . . . Ah! if I had to drink out of a cup like that! . . . Ah, my children, when I am old, good for nothing, dependent upon you, give me a pill."

"You shall have it," says Marinette. "It's a promise. Let's go and have a little chat in my room."

And maman is compelled to get up and follow her. It is all planned like a formal function.

"And you, my Jules, you're all right?"

"Pretty good."

"That's fine!"

Outside, she kisses Marinette and thanks her. It bothers me. I am not moved. It is the situation that troubles me; it is not my mother. Ah! that old woman whom later on I shall resemble. Gray hair that is still wavy. The flesh is going. The skin lies, as well as it can, on the bones, and what an importance these have taken on! The skin has scab-like spots, like unrenewed paint on old wood.

She is becoming bent. When I stand, I no longer see her terrible eyes. Sometimes, still, a pale flash reaches up to me, but the lightning of the past is gone.

Landscape. Little calves tumbling down, as though spilled out of a toy box. White cows and oxen in a field of pure green, roofs rose-colored in the setting sun, a blue sky-line, trees that as yet have only a greenish down.

A blackbird in a white cherry-tree.

A boy from the orphan asylum, hired out near Cervon, at thirteen. He is a little deaf. He receives one hundred twenty francs for fifteen months. I am thoughtless enough to say it is not much. Whereupon, lifting his eyes, which he had kept lowered, he says with pride:

"There's something else too. You get your washing done, and a pair of shoes."

MAY

Yesterday, Monday, a post-election day, Philippe drank like a calf. In the evening, I sent him to buy the paper. He did the errand all wrong, and answered me back in a thickened voice. The next day, I passed him without saying good-morning. After lunch, he comes to me as I sit under the filbert bushes.

"Monsieur, may I go and plant our potatoes?"

"Go ahead!"

He takes three steps and comes back.

"Monsieur, we had some unfavorable words last night."

"What?"

"Well, yes! I say you and I, we had some unfavorable words, because I had a drop to drink. Everybody was stopping me to buy me a drink and ask me if you were satisfied."

"That was no reason for getting yourself in that condition!"

"I'm not saying, but."

"Go on, plant your potatoes."

He takes three steps, then:

"Well, listen, find someone else to take my place. I see all right it can't go on like that. The other day you bawled me out on account of one paper, last night for another paper, two times in not many days. So, take your time: a week, two weeks, a month if you like. I don't want to leave you in the lurch, but . . ."

"You don't know what you're saying."

"That's the way it is."

He goes away.

Poor man! For a bout of drinking, he would put himself and his wife out to starve. And as for me, it's as if I'd been hit with a fist.

Marinette breaks the news to Ragotte, who is not supposed to know anything. The poor woman will be crushed! Not at all! She knows, but she says that a man with a drink in him doesn't count: he will come back.

Exhausting scene, easy to act, impossible to transcribe, in which, in front of Ragotte seated, I call Philippe, who keeps his hat on his head, a heartless man, a bad citizen, and a drunkard. He wants to leave.

"I'm not through," I say.

"Oh, me, I'm through."

"Wait. We have your situation to straighten out. So I haven't the right to reproach you when you drink?"

"Oh, yes. You have the right to say anything you like to a servant."

"You know very well I've always treated you as a friend."

I riddle him with words, and he ends up appearing not to listen, but to be watching, through the window, a rat passing by. Ragotte keeps her head down and doesn't say a word. She has understood only one thing, and says it at the end:

"So it's in October we'll have to leave?"

My heart feels hard. I speak badly, the words don't come out, and I am furious with this angry man who doesn't have a word of regret. He hangs on to his idea: as though I too had been drinking, we exchange words of about equal value.

"You tell me to talk with people! I can't talk without having a drink."

"Good. So what are you going to do?"

"We had work before we came here! We'll work again."

But he is sixty and he is deaf. I refrain from reminding him.

And not distressed at all! It would seem that they are tired of being well off: they would like a change. They thirst for some miserable freedom. He stands there like a proud lump of earth. Ragotte's head hangs–from dejection, from sleep, or from not caring, there's no telling which.

Liquidation. We shall sell the cow, kill the dogs, lose the cats, and put the key under the door. La Gloriette is dying. There are land-scapes that die like people one loves.

Philippe with a pale face and moisture in his eyes. Everything is melting.

"It isn't us that gets mad," he says. "It's the others' fault."

"Nobody has ever told me anything against you."

"Well, you say things, and then you're sorry. I'll stay as long as you want."

"All right, go to madame and tell her you regret what you said, and that I'll explain to her."

"I don't mind."

"Shake."

He finds Marinette and tells her:

"Monsieur told me to tell you that I regret what I said."

Then Ragotte kisses Marinette and says:

"For me, you are just like my mother."

Her mother is dead, and would be eighty.

"You look like you are twenty," she adds.

And La Gloriette reappears, fresh, intimate, inseparable from us.

I have become lazy because Marinette didn't dare point out to me that I was not working.

My eyes are bigger than my stomach, and my stomach is so small that it is quite enough for me to appropriate things through my eyes. Nothing for my stomach, but my eyes take in everything.

The life of a cat asleep. From time to time, a leap, a slash of claws, a stretch that resembles action, then everything returns into its fur and goes back to sleep.

Laziness: the habit of resting before fatigue sets in.

A vulgar word, which would leave an individual cold, transports a crowd.

Honorine lived so long that her death passed unnoticed. Sometimes, I think I still hear her step in the garden.

JUNE

Guitry passes through Chaumot.

I take him to see the house of Poil de Carotte. He looks at the chicken shed, the rabbit hutch, Poil de Carotte's shelter near the flow of dishwater, which I had forgotten.

"It is good," he says, "that Poil de Carotte came out of here, and that he comes back to it."

All those rosaries, those holy virgins, those photographs of first-communicants, that are an insult to the memory of papa . . .

Guitry and his fear of any insect, even a June bug.

I say: "Ah! Venice! . . ."

"Let's go there!" he says.

I refuse, but he, who had not thought about it, goes.

I ask him to take Marinette with us to Nevers.

"It is not too much? You were not planning on picking up anyone on the way?"

He lifts his arms to heaven.

He looks like an Englishman, even a graying Englishman, but he is happier if he is told that he looks like an American.

Marinette as inseparable from her needle as a bird from its beak.

You feel a certain boredom in Flaubert's work.

I am a socialist, but I turn into a furious landowner when the kids throw sticks into my cherry trees; and immediately talk of going for my gun.

Contortions of a big caterpillar assaulted by ants that climb over it, eat its head, its belly, its eyes. Gulliver in Lilliput. Its desperate efforts: it stiffens and unbends itself like a bow. Last spasm: it is dead. The ants that were afraid come running. It is black and swarming. They drag it under a strawberry plant.

I may be my age and a mayor: when I see a policeman I am uneasy.

"New poets." Remember that term, for you will not hear from them again.

JULY

Maman's real reason for corning here is to see me. She does not manage to see me, and when she leaves, she has tears in her eyes. She thanks Marinette, and, since she did not have what she wanted, digs her nails into Marinette's hand.

I have become short, tight, shrunken, owing to success, compliments. My real nature was perhaps to be light, effusive, witty. The only things I write well are letters to Marinette.

AUGUST

The exhausting horror of the ever-present sun.

The vitality of the cat, who appears so lazy. His ears and his eyes are always at work. He has within him prepared leaps, and, under him, ready claws.

As a man, Christ was admirable. As God, one could say of him: "What? Was that all He could do?"

They are not envious of the people in the château, but of the neighbor who has got on.

The day-dream: the ivy of thought which it smothers.

Walk through the fields. And you say something a little sentimental to Marinette, and suddenly you notice, on the other side of the hedge, a peasant who has overheard and looks embarrassed.

Read again old letters I wrote to Marinette. You don't change. Migraines, fury of work, bouts of laziness, a taste for life, and Marinette in the center of everything.

What surprises me is that I did not give more details. Today my eye would have taken in everything. My apparatus is better. But you become aware that you have, after all, lived, and that it is natural for life to pass and, even, for it to end.

Marinette has given me everything. Can I say that I gave her everything? It would seem that my selfishness has remained intact.

When I say to her: "Tell me frankly . . ." she reads very well in my eyes just how far she should go.

To her, I can say: "My works . . . my quality . . . my wit," even, after a tiny hesitation, . . . "my talent." She finds this manner of talking so natural that I use it without any constraint at all!

Sometimes, when she is looking at her children, she seems so close to them that they could be two of her branches.

At the thought that, through me, she might fall into want, I experience a pang; and then, too quickly, I tell myself: "How well she would stand it! And she would love me even more."

"I know what I've got," she says, "and I would change places with no woman."

Our dream dashes itself against the great mystery like a wasp against a window pane. Less merciful than man, God never opens the window.

Trip to Mont-Sabot through Combres, Ruages, Moissy; return through Mont-Bué, Lormes, Bailly, Reunebourg, Corbigny. I spread out my memory like a map and strive to see again what I have seen: and am continually astonished.

Two square-turreted châteaux that, spreading out, gradually soften into farms.

Chitry-Mont-Sabot with its straw roofs and its beautiful walnut trees. It doesn't look it, says the carter, but it's rich country. As dowry, a girl may bring a walnut tree.

Mont-Sabot. A wooden shoe with a split nose. Linden trees: one of them, struck by lightning, is dead. The church, covered with flat stones, is closed. Old tombstones, among which the oldest are the most elaborately carved. Magnificent view: Montenoison, the castle of Vauban, the immense barn at Vézelay; Lormes. To see all that, the dead need only raise themselves on an elbow.

An open country, easy to comprehend: a knoll, a dale, a knoll, a dale. From one slope to another, the peasants can watch each other work. This is the first church I feel like getting into: it is closed.

A path lies around a knoll like a garter above a knee.

Then, the rose-colored hour, the tender hour, the divine hour comes. It is a surprise that God prepares for us each evening. One should lie down in all these fields, drink all this freshness, die everywhere.

To be born here, at the foot of Mont-Sabot, what a childhood for a poet!

Small town. The daughters of the ironmonger refuse to mix with the daughters of the woman who owns the pastry shop. Iron is more noble than pastry; and besides, *they* are never seen working in the store!

A goose balanced on its two feet. The big white behind is very heavy, but the neck is long enough to balance it.

Walk in the little wood. Sniff the scent of mowed hay. On the road, a blackbird hops along in front of me as though inviting me to follow it.

Trees stopped on the hillock, like ladies watching the sunset from under their parasols.

Walk to Montenoison. Wonderful view, especially to the north. Le Morvan slightly misted over.

On this height, trees, a field of wheat, a cow, a goat. And, always, the cemetery full of its little vanities: enormous tombstones. How much effort is expended on the dead! Two women in mourning come and kneel on a grave.

The church is closed. Slightly fearful pleasure in walking over the dead.

With pride, you climb an old wall. Villages at its foot: Noison, Arthel, Champlin, and Champallement perched above a small abyss. Surprise at seeing pretty houses and, in a garden, a gentleman in a white waistcoat.

What is the use of travel! There is nature, life, history, everywhere.

Agricultural fair at Lormes. The venerable heads of reactionaries who have nothing left but the pride of being rich.

The handsome wooden horses that carry round and round first gay, then resigned human faces.

The village under the moonlight like furniture under its dustcover.

The gentle melancholy brought on by an air played on the piano is about all the sadness I have.

SEPTEMBER

That devil of a moon! What poetry it gives out!

God, in His modesty, does not dare brag of having created the world.

Philippe is returning to the earth. It is rising in him and reaching his heart. He still has human speech, but its sense is escaping him.

The details of life have paralyzed me as ivy might.

The profession of letters is, after all, the only one in which one can make no money without being ridiculous.

The moments during which, like a fish in the water, I move with ease within the infinite.

To romanticize the peasant is almost an insult to his misery. The peasant has no story; at least no romantic story.

Disgust with the literary métier, with life bent to fit the written rule, with truth amended for the reader.

These notes are my daily prayer.

When I am not original, I am stupid.

On her way to take in the cow, Ragotte crosses in front of me as I sit on a bench. She wants to say something: you do not pass in front of people without saying something.
    "I bet you the days are leaving off!" she says.

For a second, on one foot, she waits for an answer.

I don't answer. She goes off as though she were out of kilter.

The monsieur did not answer: why the—?

The onion, blown-up and bellying like those clowns with thirty-six waistcoats.

It is not necessary to live, but it is necessary to live happily.

I may not be too badly armed to deal out blows, but I am badly protected to receive them. As much through vanity as through vexation, at the first insult I fall silent.

Jesus Christ had a great deal of talent.

The sun rises before I do, but I go to bed after it does: we are even.

Everything moves in the wind, except the feeding ox, his nose firmly attached to the ground.

The clear window through which, every instant, my eyes go roaming.

Night settles in the woods; it will even spend the day there.

Five o'clock in the evening. Silent, slow struggle between shadow and sun. Shadow gains ground. The trees have it up to their waists, their crests still in the light. At the top of the field, the oxen dazzling with whiteness.

Ten o'clock in the morning is the grave and fragrant hour when the bay-leaf, the stalk of celery, the turnip, the sprigs of thyme and parsley, the leek, the clove of garlic, the onion, and the two carrots split into fourths, are assembled in the pot around the calf's head wrapped in a white cloth.

OCTOBER

Autumn. The premature age of certain trees in the midst of others that had seemed to be of the same age but have remained green.

The great, almost painful shudder that only moves us common folks, but which inspires men of genius to utter their most beautiful lamartinian cries.

Observe nature, but keep calm, like a hunter lying in wait. Things are fearful. Our emotion upsets nature. The slightest fit of bad temper frightens it. A glance weighted with too much curiosity, and life stops.

On the horizon, the moon, like a balloon unencumbered by a basket, says: "Let go!" It rises. All the cables are cut.
    Not a man, not a tree, not a dry branch was able to hang on to its net and unawares rise too.
    The red woods burn under it and inflate it.
    It reaches a cloud, seems caught, stops moving.
    It disappeared behind a mass of clouds. It was never seen again. Not that moon, at least.

Since I wear the ribbon of the Legion of Honor, I don't mind carrying Marinette's shopping net, full of cabbages, spinach, and lettuce, at the market in Corbigny.

Envious at times, I have never had the patience to be ambitious.

A girl passes along the canal. From their boat, the mariners call to her:
    "Come on over and help us eat our soup!"
    She replies, with tranquil good humor, that she hasn't the time.

That, in the evening, is as beautiful as anything that nature can arrange with trees, water, soft air, and human voices. It is infinitely sensuous.

Furious because his wife is sick and he has to wait on himself, he acts as though he did not know her when you inquire about her.

The beauty of new things, after all, is that they are clean.

Oh! Old rubbish! Old letters, old clothes, old objects that one does not want to throw away. How well nature has understood that, every year, she must change her leaves, her flowers, her fruit and her vegetables, and make manure out of the mementoes of her year!

As soon as one stops working, one feels as though one had never worked.

NOVEMBER

Not to be a man who examines his village with a magnifying glass.

Let us not forget that the world makes no sense.

What happens to all the tears we do not shed?

I am the owner of a beautiful window on nature.

Baïe does not know a single date of history, but she does know that, on 17 July 1903, the hippopotamus Tako killed his keeper.

Thadée Natanson tells me:
  "There is a gentleman who wants to put some of your *Histoires naturelles* to music. He is an avant-garde composer of whom much

is thought and for whom Debussy is old hat. How does the idea impress you?"

    "It does not impress me at all."

    "But it must mean something to you!"

    "Not at all."

    "What shall I say to him for you?"

    "Whatever you like. Thank him."

    "You don't want him to let you hear some of his music."

    "Oh no, no!"

I am not sincere, not even when I say that I am not.

Most men have seen approximately the same things, but only the artist knows how to recall them to his memory.

Paris. Anxiety upon going out the first time. A letter-box fastened to a gas lamp: never in the world will I put my letter in there. I go looking for another one.

The friends one is very fond of and never thinks about.

I am in no great hurry to see the society of the future: ours is helpful to writers. By its absurdities, its injustices, its vices, its stupidities, it feeds a writer's observation. The better men will become, the more colorless man will be.

The saddest moments: when we begin to wonder if wisdom is not just a hoax.

Speaking in public. It is not necessary to think what one says, but to think about what one says: this is harder.

You have read everything, but they have read a book that you ought to read, that makes them superior, and that annuls all you have read.

My books are so far removed from me that, already, I am a sort of posterity for them. Here is my verdict plain: I shall never read them again.

Invisible fingers stroke the smoke back, like hair, over the roof of the house.

DECEMBER

This is a notebook of abortions.

One could say of Maupassant that he died of fright. The sense of the void made him lose his head and killed him. Nowadays we are less preoccupied with the void. We are getting used to it, and this evolution within our lives is a literary revolution.

The void yields up nothing. You have to be a great poet to make it ring.

The images of Shakespeare are less literary than those of Victor Hugo, but they are more human. With Victor Hugo, you often come to see nothing but the image; with Shakespeare, you never cease to see the truth, the muscles and the blood of truth.

One should acquire a taste for Shakespeare late in life, when one has become tired of perfection.

Fantec will soon be thinking: "What a child my father is!"

A young girl told him: "On Sunday I went to the Théâtre Français. They were playing *Le Plaisir de rompre* and *Les Mouettes*. It was lovely."

"And you didn't tell her that you—knew the author of *Le Plaisir de rompre*."

"No."

I shall have to resign myself to love my son out of family feeling, because he has the brain of a stranger. Not only is he not an artist, but he works—and works too hard—for reasons that I cannot follow. He does not even impress me as being fond of work.

I have never yet used the word "coruscation."

An honorable man of talent is as rare as a man of genius.

Poil de Carotte. Still and all, I did not dare write everything. I did not tell this: M. Lepic sending Poil de Carotte to ask Mme. Lepic if she wanted a divorce, and Mme. Lepic's reception. What a scene!

A pretty woman is permitted less delicacy of ear than of tongue. She may hear coarse language: she must not use it.

There is a justice, but we do not always see it. Discreet, smiling, it is there, at one side, a little behind injustice, which makes a big noise.

Through the door of the north, wide open, freed clouds spread over the world.

I spend my days at my desk like a hare in his burrow. I dream, and, like him, I am fearful—fearful of writing.

I have come to the age where I can understand how deeply I must have annoyed my masters when I went to see them and never talked to them about themselves.

Sarah is no longer an actress. She is something like the song of trees, like the monotonous sound of an instrument. It is perfect, and we are used to it.

Every time I want to settle down to work, literature gets between.

In the evening, when Marinette, after a good day filled with work, listens to her children, looks at one, then at the other, never missing a thing, she is beautiful, she has something holy about her.

With a single glance, she takes in their entire life, of which she remembers every detail.

I have an idea the way I look at a bird: I am always afraid it will fly away, and I don't dare touch it.

Snow. The village sleeps under a white night.

1907

*. . . one does not grow old. Where the heart is concerned, the fact
is accepted, at least in matters of love. Well, it is the same with the
mind, it always remains young. You do not understand life
any more at forty than you did at twenty, but you are
aware of this fact, and you admit it.
To admit it is to remain young.*

In February, JR begins writing for the daily, *Messidor*, theater notes, dramatic criticism, short stories (later to be assembled under the title, *Nos Frères Farouches*). JR
elected to the Académie Goncourt. Re-issue of *Poil de Carotte* by Calmann-Lévy.

JANUARY

To tell the truth, I feel that things are passing, that the end is taking
shape, over there in the fog, and that I must take advantage of what
may be left. If I want to do something, the time is now.

M. Ravel, the composer of *Histoires naturelles*, dark, rich, distinguished, was very insistent that I go this evening to listen to the melodies he has written.

I explained my ignorance and asked him to tell me what it was he could add to *Histoires naturelles*.

"My intention was not to add anything," he said, "but to interpret them."

"But what connection . . . ?"

"To say with music what you would say with words when you are in front of a tree, for example. I think and I feel in music, and I should like to think and feel the same things you do. There is instinctive, sentimental music, such as mine—needless to say, the craft must first be learned—and intellectual music, such as that of d'Indy. This evening there will be practically only d'Indy's. Some composers do not admit emotion because they do not want to explain it. I believe the opposite; but these others must be interested in what I am doing, since they admit me. This test is extremely important to me. One thing I am sure of is my singer: she is marvelous." [This was Jane Bathori. JR did not go, but sent his wife and daughter.]

Nest for rent. Water and sun on every branch.

FEBRUARY

To work at no matter what; that is, to be a critic.

In gilt-edged books, says Baïe, there is always someone called Anselme.

I understand life less and less, and love it more and more.

To the young. I shall tell you a truth that you may not like, because you look forward to novelty. This truth is that one does not grow old. Where the heart is concerned, the fact is accepted, at least in matters of love. Well, it is the same with the mind. It always remains young. You do not understand life any more at forty than you did at twenty, but you are aware of this fact, and you admit it. To admit it is to remain young.

Trip to Chaumot. Nature drenched. They all have red faces, their blood gone to the head. They keep warm in each other's houses.

Philippe's fingers tremble as he touches a sheet of paper. I would like to talk softly to him, but, because he is getting deaf, I must shout. I sound as though I were in a temper.

He is so cold he has lost his smell. His beard is frozen by the cold that comes down the chimney.

In the vegetable garden, the indomitable leek never freezes.

The only water that does not freeze is that in the well.

A poplar sways like a long pole.

The magpie passes, like a crow in half-mourning.

How would they manage to bring up their children if death did not help them?

They have a certain savour when one visits them between trains. They are close to nature, as close to the soil as their animals. They live the silent life of leeks, and one marvels that they do not freeze.

I love music, all kinds of music, the most simple as well as the most complicated, the kind that so generously permits us to go on thinking of something else. It makes me think of the swaying of the poplars in my village, minus their leaves; and the canal where, at the behest of a wind without pretensions, the reeds bend and rise like violin-bows in an orchestra, but with less noise.

The writer of prose is supposed not to need music. This is not at all the case; without it he would be nothing.

The conductor translates the music by means of the precise pantomime of a great actor, receives sudden blows in the solar plexus, picks a note out of the air, says "hush" with his finger to his lips, lunges forward, takes a dance step, bars the horizon with his extended stick, drops his arms: it is finished.

Your heart, which you had believed to be dry to the point of hearing it crackle, suddenly spills over with tears.

MARCH

At the agricultural fair.

The poetry of machines. One of them rubs its little fists together before smashing them into your face; another has a great maw with five or six tongues that alternately rise and fall.

Lunch at the Café Anglais with Téry, Jouvenel [who married Colette in 1912], Monzie, and Tristan [Bernard]. The question is of doing some work for *Le Matin*. Nothing could be less tempting.

Jouvenel, delicate features, delicate mustaches, asks me for articles on general subjects. What a choice! He directs *Le Matin*, almost all of France, a part of the world; it is very funny.

"Send me whatever you like," he says, "of any length you like. I don't want to be, in Paris, the man who will have cut Jules Renard's writing."

Téry contributes an article a day. A few of them go in, and they are cut! and cut! This young professor is getting acquainted with the beauties of journalism.

APRIL

When a sparrow has said "Peep!", it thinks it has said everything there is to say.

I have a remarkable memory: I forget everything! It is wonderfully convenient. It is as though the world were constantly renewing itself for me.

Monday. People waken. The first day of the week always has something of a day of birth.

Rabelais is a man of gaiety, not of wit.

Going through the Tuileries, I feel emotional because children play and birds sing. I am moved because a statue with broken toes shows the iron rods in its feet.

MAY

I like the common flower and the rare compliment.

A young man without talent is an old man.

JUNE

Chaumot. At the school, the children all stand up when I come in, except one. He is on strike. He remains seated, his head propped on his elbow.

The quail plays with little stones and thinks it is singing.

The goldfinch: the jewel among birds.

Philippe feels dull every Sunday. He says so, and he yawns, but he would not go out and burn out a nest of caterpillars.

To make their lunch, Ragotte pours a pot of water into yesterday's broth. Then she goes to sit and think at the foot of the old cross.

It is possible to work in one's study, with the window open, until eight o'clock. It is possible.

We are in the world to laugh.

In purgatory or in hell we shall no longer be able to do so.

And in heaven it would not be proper.

Death is the normal state. We make too much of life.

JULY

The world would be happy if it were upside down.

It is more difficult to be an honorable man for eight days than a hero for fifteen minutes.

M. Roy [the schoolmaster of Chitry], so respectful that, when I hypocritically say something derogatory about myself, he does not contradict me.

The fields of wheat in which partridges have their little streets.

Marinette at once angelic and demoniac in the midst of her preserving-pans.

A man who would have an *absolutely clear* vision of the void would kill himself immediately.

A gold thimble is the finest present you could make to Marinette.

"Oh, you carry a basket?" says she to Marinette. She, herself, will go to market, but not without her maid.

The notary's wife will not go without her veil.

There is a young girl who goes in an embroidered dress, barely touches things; and soon, in a flurry, begins to lift her feet: "Oh! Chickens! Geese!"

A farmer's wife, who has made sacrifices so that her son can study medicine, is not too proud to come and sell a pound of butter. She is dressed up, wearing jewelry. When she is asked: "How much a pound, madame?" the answer comes out of a pinched-up hen's bottom:

"Thirty sous, madame."

AUGUST

After seeing what the bourgeois crave, I feel myself capable of doing without everything.

The old woman has got into the habit of coming to sit on the bench. There is another who will take her place, full size, in one of my books!

I must let things take time to settle on my memory, like objects of art on a well balanced table.

Last night, a first peal of thunder. Philippe goes to fetch the donkey in the field, and I, Baïe in her bed.

Immense sky. Clouds will never be able to fill it.

Pay no attention to the truth. Then it will leap out at you.

The comet of August 1907. You spot it very quickly in the east, probably by two o'clock in the morning. It looks like a pale shooting star arrested as it falls on the Narteau woods; also like a billiard cue flung into the sky.

With my lantern, my red dressing gown, my wool shawl, and my visored cap on top of a cotton nightcap, I must look like an old astrologer without his spectacles.

Fortunately, a cloud covers up the comet. Nothing is more monotonous than these marvels.

All that does not prove the devil.

On the horizon, shortly before the sun, a star—Saturn or Jupiter—riscs. It is well worth a comet.

One must write as one speaks, if one speaks well.

The automobile, vertiginous boredom.

SEPTEMBER

Ragotte wistfully watches the threshing. Her youth as a sturdy harvest girl buzzes in her ears. She now begins some of her tales with: "At the time I was doing the harvest . . ."

Trip to the Provence with Guitry

The sun makes me sing.
Too few road signs, approaching Marseilles.
"You are about to see the most beautiful road in the world," says Marius, the chauffeur. "Not a single tree."
Torrents of white stone.
Thanks to the speed, we are not too hot. As soon as we stop, the sun machine-guns us.
Le Puy. They are a little ashamed of their gilded Virgin, and tell us that one gets used to her.

I want to do things right, and that someone, anyone, should take note of it.

Mountains unrolling.
Figs, green lemons, cicadas. An eagle drops.
Butter already smelling of oil.
And it is again Guitry who gets all the attention from the tarts on the Marseilles streets.

There are women who work. Not all women are idle.
This one saved her husband a servant and a handyman. She was always ill-tempered because she could never get her work done. She died of it.
That one, worn out, is sitting, almost lying, on the embankment. It is the end! She has no strength left. She says:
"The peasant is too miserable. Why are there any?"

Her face is resigned, almost mean. Her husband, a stacker, earns good money. She might have been happy with him, but he drinks, and beats her. She sees nothing of what he earns. She gives up.

Still, on the fourth page of a newspaper, she has seen an advertisement that will perhaps make her get back her strength. She is going to take *les Pilules Pink*. This is her last hope. Who would take it from her?

I never know a thing; so I always have the pleasure of learning no matter what comes along.

The truth of the spider is the fly.

My brain is becoming like a spider's web; life can no longer go by without being caught.

September evening. The light sound of the mill. A lantern hurries past. On the boats, the lights go out.

A sudden cry, coming from one knows not where. But nobody is being murdered. A natural cry, perhaps; that is, from nature.

Unperturbed as an ox who could not be sold at the fair.

At four o'clock, Ragotte stuffs herself with bread. Standing in the court, she holds a salt cellar in one hand and dips a cucumber into it.

"My bread was too old," she says. "It didn't give me any appetite. The cucumber and the salt will push it along."

They don't see themselves at all. They would not recognize themselves in *Frères Farouchaes*. They would say: "Well, what of it? those things happen to everybody."

Evening. A soul is wandering; you can hear its little bell.

Ragotte, sixty-two years old, but possessed of all her appetite.

Her vanity lies in wanting to make one believe that women eat less than men. At noon, she eats less than Philippe, but she doesn't say that, at ten o'clock, she was standing in the court putting away a slice of bread and cheese four centimeters thick.

On Sunday, she prepares tiny little lunches for Philippe, because he doesn't work.

Automobiles on the road, hunters in the fields, the earth is becoming uninhabitable.

The poet. Like the cicada: a single note indefinitely repeated.

What visitors admire most in my home country is not me: it is the whiteness of our oxen.

An autumn butterfly, forgetting itself, lives on.

In the path, the caterpillar plays a soundless little tune on its accordion.

Paris

Académie Goncourt. There are more than thirty candidates [for the vacancy created by the death of J.K. Huysmans].

OCTOBER

The theatre. To think that God, who sees everything, must see that!

I tell Baïe to fetch me my notebook and pencil.
    "Right away," says she. "Hang on to your idea, Papa!"

Every day, I am a child, a man, an oldster.

Last night, returning home at six o'clock, I find in my study Mirbeau and Thadée.

"Your election is certain," Mirbeau tells me. "We have your five votes."

"May I say that I am very happy?"

"No. There is first a necessary formality: you must declare your candidacy. It is required by the statutes of the Council of State. Hennique would like me to bring him a word from you: he will vote for you. Mme. Daudet told him that Léon would vote for you. Certainly, by the second ballot, you will have your five votes. Descaves has said to Hennique: 'If there were 150 ballots, I would vote 150 times for Renard.'"

"But," I say, "I have criticized the Goncourts. That will be brought up."

"Bah," replies Mirbeau, "I wrote that I never read them any more."

Worried all day. Suddenly, a desire to weep, like a man overwhelmed with happiness and without courage to stand up to it.

And, at every instant, I fall into poses, theatrical remarks.

Sleep badly. At five o'clock, I begin to wait. Nothing this morning. Not a letter, not a newspaper that says anything pleasant.

Marinette is gay. She is a little surprised at me. Truly, I am ridiculous, and annoyed at myself.

Night of the 24th to the 25th spent walking around, looking at my watch, looking out of the window. The thing is bereft of all sense. There is nothing to do but go to bed, where, knocked out, I fall asleep at once.

In the morning, wake up early. Suppose I have been elected after all? The first paper, *Le Figaro*, informs me that there were no results:

"In spite of the efforts of Messrs. Descaves and Mirbeau on behalf of M. Jules Renard . . . etc. etc." Other papers say that Victor Margueritte had four votes, Céard three, I, two.

. . . I am trying to rest when Paul Margueritte arrives. The second time a member of the Academy has called on me. . . . He tells me he is broken-hearted to vote against me, but that he is bound to his brother. . . . We part good friends.

Telegram from Mirbeau, followed by his visit, in the evening, with Thadée. [Report on the ballotting]. It was becoming exciting. Justin Rosny declared:

"My brother and I are ready to go over to Renard, but he needs a fifth vote." Silence. Finally, Hennique said:

"All right. I'll do it."

"In that case," said Justin Rosny, "Renard should have unanimity. An artist of his stature should be well received."

But Léon Daudet said to Hennique who had picked up his pen:

"What? You are deserting us?"

And—fateful moment!—Hennique was seen to hesitate. He, too, was broken-hearted. Suddenly he said:

"No, No! A thirty years' friendship—I can't. My vote must go to Céard."

Everything was back where it started. The meeting was adjourned.

I was covered with bouquets by everyone. Even Léon Daudet said nothing against me.

"But Céard is partner in a dive!" said Mirbeau.

"We do not look into private lives," replied Daudet.

"Couldn't we find someone who could make us agree? A poet, for instance?" said Bourges.

"Who?" asked Mirbeau.

Bourges could think of no one.

Descaves sends me word to have patience for another week.

No! I don't want to play either the part of the gent who hangs on or the one who sacrifices himself. And then, truly! having been honorary victor of this day, having won the votes of the Rosnys, which I cared about, I find my balance restored, and, truly, down deep, it doesn't matter any more.

But, let's admit it, all this publicity amuses me.

The Académie Goncourt seems sick; it seems like a home for old friends. Literature will lose interest in it.

If we were able to, I shall not say capture for ever, but prolong, the minutes of emotion experienced through music, we should be more than men.

To love music is to make sure of at least one fourth of one's happiness.

I stopped in the middle of a field like a man suddenly hearing beautiful, solemn music.

I promise fifty francs to Fantec after he will have passed his examination.

"What will you buy with it?"

"A skull."

I tell Mirbeau and Descaves that I want to withdraw. Descaves protests; Mirbeau does too, but not so much. Victor Margueritte is supposed to have said: "Renard is yielding to me." Hennique has pulled the blankets over his head.

NOVEMBER

Returning home at midnight after dinner at the Brandès's, we find the following card, which the concierge gets out of bed to give us: "This time, you're in! Lucien Descaves, Octave Mirbeau, J. & H. Rosny."

I shall ask for a raise in salary.

This evening, first Goncourt dinner.

I was deeply disappointed when my sponsors would not let me make a speech. As you see, I have prepared nothing . . .

I am proud to be one of the heirs of Goncourt. He might not, if he saw me, send down a malediction upon me. I am less sure where Huysmans is concerned . . .

I devote much of my life to dreaming, being lazy. I shall have to watch myself a little hereafter . . .

The dinner is ordered.

We eat horrible stuff. Why do we have to dine like snobs? Is Elémir Bourges, that thin little man, poor and buttoned up, going to eat a sixteen-franc dinner with a two-franc tip, and perhaps smoke a cigar that will cost over a franc?

DECEMBER

Love, which fills only a small corner of life, occupies the whole stage at the theatre.

Anger wears you out. If you aren't careful in this regard, the boors might soon kill you off.

Walks. The body advances, while the mind flutters around it like a bird.

1908

*Books have lost their savour. They no longer teach me anything.
It is as though one were to suggest to a painter that he copy a
painting. O nature! There is only you left.*

JR writes a one-act play, *Le Cousin de Rose*, based on an episode in *Ragotte*. Part of
Ragotte appears in *La Grande Revue*. *Mots d' Ecrit* and *Ragotte* published.

JANUARY

Moments when even the man who is least modest is astonished to
find that he is something.

A single experience has gathered strength in me: everything depends
on work. To work we owe everything; it is the great regulator of
life.

A window on the street is as good as a stage.

I should like to see someone sadder than myself; the animals in the
zoo, for instance.

I feel romantic for a few minutes a day; no woman profits by it.

If my books bore painters as much as their paintings bore me, I forgive them.

Writing for someone is like writing to someone: you immediately feel obliged to lie.

Poetry saved me from the foul sickness of maliciousness.

There is also a sort of deliberate originality, which one expects, which becomes commonplace, and which leaves one cold.

Voltaire was a wonderful business man, which explains why he did not remain the poet he believed himself to be.

Shadow lives only in light.

A cloud sails along as though it knew where it was going.

The enormous and useless Bonnefon. What a handsome monk he would have made!

The danger of success is that it makes us forget the world's dreadful injustice.

Taste ripens at the expense of happiness.

It should not be thought that laziness is unproductive. Within it, you live intensely, like a hare listening. You swim in it as in water; and are brushed by the grasses of self-reproach.

Oh, for something new! Something new, if it consist of my death!

The naturalists, like Maupassant, observed a little of life and filled in the rest.

As for us, we no longer dare arrange anything. We count on life to complete life. If life is in no hurry, we wait.

To them, life was not sufficiently literary. To us, it is beautiful enough.

Mme. de Noailles has a good spoken press. She is a woman of genius.

She is the only woman who does not copy men, says Rosny.

And the only one, I say, who is not afraid of ridicule.

A young black-haired chap, of flourishing mien, plump, soft, and perhaps all of eighteen, comes to see me. He had let me know by letter that he would call in order to inquire into the genesis of Poil de Carotte.

He looks stupid; I don't see what he is trying to do, I have not the slightest interest in having him do it or in seeing him again, and I tell him everything, everything! And I become animated, and I explain things well. For nothing, I cast one of my best pages into the lap of this unknown.

Ah, no! I am not one of those who need to go to Venice in order to experience an emotion.

My life gives the impression of being in harmony with itself, and yet I have done almost nothing of what I wanted to do.

FEBRUARY

Every morning, upon waking, you should say: "I see, I hear, I move, I am not in pain. Thank you! Life is lovely."

Life is what our character makes it. We fashion it, as a snail does its shell. A man can say: "I never made a fortune because it is not in my character to be rich."

Collectivism! Talent can be nothing but individual.

It is easier to be generous than not to regret it afterwards.

Chaumot

[Peasants.] They have two kinds of diseases: those of the blood, and pains. It is the blood that goes to the head, that stops at the throat, or that belabors the loins. The women talk of change of life by thirty; their blood is working on them.

Philippe, proud of knowing a spring no one else knows. He doesn't tell.

They have no idea how long a cow can live. As soon as they think she may be old, they fatten her and sell her to the butcher.

Tomorrow I shall be forty-four. That is no age. It is only at forty-five that one must begin to think; forty-four is a year of velvet.

There is no note, last year, on my being forty-three; it didn't frighten me.

Forty-four is the age at which you must begin to give up the hope of doubling your years.

I feel old, but I would not be younger by five minutes.

My ignorance and my admission of ignorance—these constitute the best part of my originality.

MARCH

Rosny says:

"Yes, I know how to construct a story. I don't snip a story out of a novel, or out of impressions; I know how to set it up in its proper frame.

"I am not ill-natured, and I change my shirt whenever my wife wants me to, but I am rather grouchy.

"I don't suffer from long spells of discouragement, but I am by nature sad, and every evening I think of death. I am in love with life, and tell myself that death is approaching. I am not afraid of it, and I know it ends everything, but I am sorry it should be necessary to die, that is, to grow old first."

To write, constantly to write! But nature does not constantly produce. She gives flowers and fruit in her season, and then she rests for at least six months. Which is about my measure.

Jules Romains [then twenty-three] author of *Bourg Régénéré*, prose, and *La Vie Humaine*, poetry, comes to call on me. Has degrees in both science and letters. Gives lessons. Has published his books at his own expense and is now trying to find a publisher for a book of prose. Fasquelle refuses to look at it.

Société des Gens de Lettres. So many people of whom I have not read a single letter! All the ugly women who say to you: "Do you think it may be an advantage to be a woman?"

Maman thinks only of taking care of herself and living another fifty years.

To read again the poetry you once knew by heart.

APRIL

Words: the pieces of change in the currency of a sentence. They must not get in the way. There is always too much small change.

Zola immoral? He stinks of morality! Coupeau is punished, Nana is punished, all Zola's bad people are punished.

A tempest blown up for the purpose of ruffling a sparrow's feathers.

I know only one truth: work alone creates happiness. I am sure only of that one thing, and I forget it all the time.

[Académie Goncourt.] Hennique is supposed to have said to des Gachons: "Victor Margueritte added nothing to us. Renard provided a new note." Did he say that before or after the election?

Philippe writes that La Gloriette is almost sold to two elderly bachelors. My destiny, already somewhat tired, is changing horses once more.

I have a morality, but it is pretty tortuous. I arrive at what's right by taking cross-cuts.

MAY

Today, visited the rectory. It is quite the kind of house a curé or a free-thinking man should live in. Windows on the river; a cistern. The garden filled with the scent of wallflowers. A shed, a stable, closets. An almost vertical roof. But it is almost under the heavy foot of the bell-tower.

The ostrich, a giant chick.

Philippe makes holes in the ground with his spade and then fills them up again. It is true he puts potatoes in them, but this doesn't seem to be important.

An old tree in bloom, almost in white hair.

Silence. I hear my ear.

How many things are too long-drawn-out! How many joys that, before finally coming to an end, smoke like an ill-trimmed wick!

It is the rich who spoil the Bois de Boulogne. And the horseback riders who delight in making their saddle creak! And the poor old men doing a bit of bicycling before they die!

The governesses sitting on benches and reading books that are always in very fine print. They are ruining their eyes.

The Bois, which at the moment could make me weep with joy, leaves me, not with a desire to return to it, but with a desire for the country.

How few there are who can look at something beautiful without thinking that they will now be able to say: "I have seen something beautiful!"

Nature quivers at being painted by a young girl.

Society of Authors. . . . Mirbeau wears a small flat hat, like a man who has definitely decided he will no longer be afraid of Claretie.

Coppée. No, no! Death is no excuse. He was a poor sort of man. You do not open a book of poetry in order to gain knowledge about humble folks. Coppée will not be opened again. If it does not augment you to read him, of what good is a poet?

Where is the modesty of this man who scorned speeches (Why? He lived by them!) and demanded military honors? How will the soul of this man who was never a soldier understand a military exercise? If at least it said: "I am not worthy of it! . . ." But no: this soul wants honors, and not such as are suitable for a man of letters. Old snob! Poet for a king who would have appointed him historiographer!

Claudel says of Jammes that he is the greatest poet of all time, and Jammes says it of Claudel.

The Abbey of Valoires, which cannot be found on the map. A lovely ruin. Woodwork, a chapel with a grille worth a great deal of money. On the ceiling, a cup fungus reminds us that there was one growing on the spot where the chapel was built. And nature covers everything once more. Flowering gardens, trees of great beauty. The way these monks understood life: to be useless.

JUNE

Men of talent who do what men of originality do not want to do.

Style. Thick, heavy syllables that deafen the reader and prevent the sentence from being heard.

Removal to Chaumot for the summer

Truth that creates illusions is the only kind I like.

Night. Suddenly, you think you hear the sound of a drum.

Fame is the smoke without fire that we hear so much about.

A sentence can only be the filter of thought.

If I were to be unfaithful to you with another woman, I should all the time be looking your way.

Storm. You don't like people who say, "It doesn't scare me." Why shouldn't they be frightened like everyone else? And you try to think of something that will make them worry.

One of the small benefits of fear: trying to buck up others.

The lily is white even at night.

The magpie in the field, the oriole, the cuckoo. Overnight, they have become more trusting. They thought man had vanished.

JULY

The tender light of morning, in which all colors appear to their advantage.

First appearance of Augustine, who is about to be involved in our life. The aspect of a solid farm girl. She came "on her feet." You wonder why she didn't bring her cow.

They all say: "You can tell me whatever you like." Augustine adds: "Me, first off, if you swear at me, I cry."

Her big, not-too-bright girl's face lights up when she says: "I'd like to see Paris!" She smiles. "I'd like to see what's in that town. Oh, not to stay there all the time; I'd come back to the country."

Ragotte's comment: "Her talk isn't quick, but she's nice."

Augustine says further: "I hurried because I know that many girls want the job in your house, and the one who left would like to come back. You can ask wherever you like. There's nothing to be said against me."

Just enough education to make a good illiterate in three or four years, when she will have forgotten what she has learned, that is, almost nothing.

A grainy face, well scrubbed with laundry soap.

She will come to us with her little bundle, into a house where there are four strangers, without counting Philippe and Ragotte who may be enemies, and it is we who take precautions against her, we who are fearful and mistrustful!

"I like her better than the other one," says Ragotte. "The other one wore too many flounces."

Books have lost their savour. They no longer teach me anything. It is as though one were to suggest to a painter that he copy a painting. O nature! There is only you left.

The arm I want to extend toward my manuscript seems to be paralyzed.

Nothing disgusts me more than my drafts of manuscripts: eggs crushed before they are laid.

AUGUST

Augustine would not have wanted to start with us yesterday, a Friday: it is a bad day. Amazed because Baïe asks her to draw a pail of water and says thank you.

She washes her feet once a week. She will wash them more often, if we like.

She is seventeen years old. She has been working for five years. At thirteen, she had twenty cows to milk on a farm.

When she was twelve, she earned forty francs a year. It was on a farm, and the kind of situation, she says, from which a girl comes out "in trouble," that is, pregnant.

Attracted and worried by Paris. She is afraid of being murdered.

"Is there an attic in which to dry the wash? You can't dry it outside in winter."

"Neither outside nor in the attic. The laundress brings it back all dry, ironed, folded."

"Then what do we do, we, the maids, in Paris?"

She has four chemises. She will buy six more with her next wages.

She asks if, in Paris, we have a cow.

"How pretty it must be there on Sunday!" she says.

"Why, it's like any other day."

"But isn't it a feast day?"

"Every day here," she says, "ever since I came, I eat something new. If I had started running the last time I had roast chicken to eat, I'd be a long way off!"

Mostly, what frightens her about Paris is the "carnival masks." It seems that there are lots, but lots of them!

Anguish that feeds on nothing.

In summer, certain evenings have the resonance of winter. Nature in error.

The bat always seems to be flying within four walls.

A note to be taken! But you can find no pencil in nature.

I have never been able to prevent myself from saving a fly caught in a spider's web.

Augustine, having got up too late, made everything right by setting the clock back three quarters of an hour.

The workman seems to be alive, if you compare him with the dead peasant.

Storm. The lightning flashes its tongues into the house and at my face.

Strangers who come to say to the people of my country that they don't know me.

SEPTEMBER

To think that, this morning, I went to the mairie on the pretense of picking up a certain paper, simply to show those officers that I wear a decoration!

And I found a colonel there wearing a full cross: serves me right!

Return to Paris

Last night, reread some Taine and Gautier. How much superior of the two is Gautier: he has the exact word, of the right color. He has words of all colors, and he knows how to select them. Besides, he does not suggest: he paints directly. Taine works hard. He is outstanding on set subjects, but posterity does not care about that sort of thing.

Even the rooster was asleep. I alone was wakeful in the night. Shadows that don't speak but resent me. Thin streak of light. A snowy reflection. People I don't know. That hand fluttering at the edge of the shutter.

At that moment the cock crows. Light. The hand is a vine leaf.

The cock's crow has echoed against the walls of my heart, and I peacefully go back to sleep.

Art: to nudge truth along a little.

"Oh, I understand that madame must be on the lookout," says Augustine, "but I would not be a thief for the sake of a pair of drawers. Madame can look: I don't wear any.

"I thought it would be uncomfortable in Paris, but I like it here. It isn't so very ugly!"

Taine wanted to have travel impressions. Gautier had them.

We have received our early ideas, formed our taste, on books of which the first page was torn off, leaving us ignorant of both title and author. It is the old, tattered novel read forty times on the sly that has left the most lasting mark on us.

A peasant's remark which illuminates a man to his very soul, as though the valves of his body had opened.

The admirations of which we are not too sure. Just a "Really, you like that?" from anyone at all is enough to throw us off. Perhaps we were wrong, after all. From there to cast our admiration overboard is child's play.

I am friendly toward people only if I feel securely superior to them.

I travel incognito, too much so.

OCTOBER

"Why should I care about your being patriots if you are dishonorable men?"

"Patriotism above all!"

"Not at all: only along with the rest. Without the rest, it is nothing."

To be a Jew, in our time, is already to be something of a celebrity.

Anatole France is really nothing but the foremost among the amateurs.

Rouché, the editor of *La Grande Revue*, calls to convey to me the compliments of his readers on *Ragotte*, and to make offers. He would like to have first option on my copy; for this he would pay me 1800 francs a year. I sense him to be foxy, hesitant, stingy, and, as for me, I am stupid with indecision and modesty, and I know it.

Then he asks me if I have ever done criticism.

Chantilly

Beautiful swans, with back too round, the rudder of the tail a little heavy and thick, but graceful and white all the same, pure white except for the red beak and the feet gloved in black like the arms of Yvette Guilbert. Carps brush the underbelly of the ducks and cause a light ripple in the water.

A peacock, self-conscious and well-trained, splendid without trying, perches on a window sill.

The banks of the stream, the Nonette, are straight as though drawn with a ruler, but the water flows. It is nature put to rights, it is no longer the forest primeval. Should we find fault with it? Should we not admire this long alley under a dome of trees? And, over there, at its end, the sun that already touches the horizon?

Here I could write a masterpiece in a month. Here, I should have much more talent, if I did not die of boredom.

It is as beautiful as Versailles, and with more variety.

Vast, empty stables, high and cool as a cathedral.

The water edged by its banks like a mirror by its frame.

Rapid, sharp-flighted ducks, bringers of messages to the reeds.

This kind of scenery can be seen in the theatre, but there it is made out of cardboard and quickly made. Here, it is made out of trees and the work of centuries.

When the defects of others are perceived with so much clarity, it is because one possesses them oneself.

It is always surprising to see a man and a woman, silent and indifferent, side by side. One forgets that perhaps they sleep together.

There are moments when everything turns out right. Don't let it alarm you: they pass.

NOVEMBER

A note must say more than a page: otherwise, it is useless.

Last night, a letter informed me that La Gloriette is almost sold. Change of direction. La Gloriette is dying. Let us hope that the book will live! It is time to retreat to my father's house. I leave *La Gloriette*. Will it be to inhabit *la gloire*?

A man of letters should be only a man of letters. All the rest is literature.

Those abominable people who write to you before having read your book!

Ragotte. It is not going like hotcakes, but it is going all the same, according to Vezier, the clerk at Floury's.

It looks as though the material success were not going to correspond with the literary success.

What most surprises me is this heart which keeps on beating.

DECEMBER

Augustine blows on an ember until it is burnt up, then thinks she has put it out.
  "I am no better than another," she says, "but I fry a good egg."
  One of these Sundays, she is boldly going to wash her hair.

In our friendships and our loves we must also be constantly deprived.

One must know how to be careless with style in order to sound more limber.

You sit down to work. For a long time, nothing. You don't even try. All at once, a sort of breath passes, and the fire catches.

At my desk I am like a donkey in his stall. I read and do nothing. My mind eats and ruminates.

Augustine, when the cauliflower au gratin appears.
  "Hey!" she cries, "are we going to live good!"
  She eats too much, digests badly, and yawns her head off. She has to take off her corset to wash the kitchen floor.

At night, she falls asleep like a log, but she has nightmares, shouts, sings, and knocks everything to the floor.

Peasants. In winter, they live asleep, stopped up like snails.

God. "He feedeth the birds of the air." And then, in winter, lets them starve.

My attitude toward peasants has been the same as toward nature, toward animals, water, trees.

What I say about a tree can be applied to all the others, but it is by looking at the one, and not at the others, that I find the image that will transmit a communicable impression to the reader.

Athis tells me:

"There are women who say, when looking at your book: 'As for me, I must admit I cannot get interested in stories about common folks.'"

Peasants. They go to bed at five o'clock, sleep until one in the morning, then wake up and lie feeling dull till daylight.

1909

I can no longer walk from one end of the Tuileries to the other.
I am obliged to sit down and give two sous to the old
women who sell lilies-of-the-valley.

Revival of *Poil de Carotte* at the *Théâtre de l' Odéon*. The play will become a part of
the repertoire of the Comédie-Française. Production of *La Bigote* at the Théâtre de
l'Odéon, a violently anti-clerical play centering around Mme. Lepic.

JANUARY

"Hey, am I going to work good!" says Augustine. "What pretty
presents! A watch, a chain! Hey, there, madame, how I love you!
I've never been gifted like today."

The man of taste tries to train himself to look down on great men.

One shouldn't run down friends: they are still the best thing we
have.

In order to read properly what one has written, one must think it again.

FEBRUARY

Augustine, feeling chilly, does the rooms with the windows closed, and shakes her dustrag over the rug.

Chaumot

Philippe is not upset by the sale of La Gloriette. He is ready to work for the next tenant. Like a cat, he is more attached to the house than to me.

When I repeat, "You need not worry about your daily bread," Ragotte, who was always so pleased when "madame Jules" came, replies:

"We do thank you."

But Philippe says nothing, as though either he does not believe me, or it were something owed him.

"I'll look after your garden up there [Chitry]", he says, "and I'll work some place else."

"Where?"

"Oh, that doesn't worry me."

"You're not a young man any more."

"One can work to the end."

"Besides, I'll always be here," I say. "You shall not want for the necessary."

He finally makes up his mind to say:

"I know monsieur will not leave me in want."

Maman moaning, buried in an armchair; but she comes to life again very quickly, her eyes sharp and furious because she can't order Marinette about.

"What a success, Jules's book!" she says. "For you people, everything comes out right."

She bought it because Amélie wrote her she couldn't find it at Saint-Etienne. She was surprised to learn that it cost only twenty-seven sous. She thought all books cost three francs.

"How cold it is this winter!"

"You have wood to keep you warm."

"Wood at forty-five francs the cord! And there's no one here to visit. The other day, I wanted to go to La Gloriette, but I was caught by a gust of wind on the bridge. I couldn't go on. It upset me, because Ragotte had sent word she'd be so happy to see me!"

Paris

A vanity so prodigious he could not have put it into verse.

A man for whom the outside world did not exist.

He believed in the common man, to whom he had never given a glance.

He was called handsome as a god. No one ever dared say he was handsome as a man.

Mendès was everything I did not like, perhaps everything I envied.

Augustine has no savings. She has spent all her money on barley sugar and illustrated serials. She is bored here. She wants to go home to her village, find work on a farm, and dance every Sunday.

A certain M. Bloch, of the *Gaulois*, asks to be presented to me in order to tell me that *Ragotte* is a masterpiece. I can think of nothing to answer, and come up with a poor:

"Oh, you liked it. I thank you."

A new maid. Marie. Believes in the number thirteen and doesn't work on Sundays. At thirty-eight, she is no more advanced than she was at thirteen. She was married once, and feels that it's enough.

She remembers only one good situation, at the Spanish embassy.

She has been in homes where the coffee was weighed out, and where her dinner consisted of a hard-boiled egg when the masters, who were rich, dined out.

She eats the crusts of the day before. She hasn't tasted fresh bread for a year. Shy, with an Alsatian accent and a lisp, she begs pardon when she crosses in front of an armchair.

Paris lighted up by snow in full daytime.

Literature is an occupation in which you have to keep proving your talent to people who have none.

Good taste may be nothing but a fear of life and a fear of the beautiful.

MARCH

There is false modesty, but there is no false pride.

[Ragotte came to Paris and stayed with her daughter and son-in-law.]

With her gloves on, Ragotte can't take hold of her handkerchief. She would rather climb the stairs than take the elevator.

She says to Lucienne, her daughter: "You didn't read monsieur's book? Me, I know it! It made me laugh good! You've got to buy it."

She is constantly afraid that the carriages will telescope into each other.

The cinema where you always think it's for real, the little seats that fold up, the sleepy little boys who seem to understand better than she does.

Antoine, always ill at ease among witty people. When he wants to say something, he makes a desperate effort, and his little eyes move closer to his nose.

One should say nothing, because everything offends.

Rain mixed with piano drops.

And now they are analyzing little bottles of my urine, and I have albumin. And, by means of a gadget halfway between a compass and a watch, Renault takes my blood pressure, and the needle shows twenty. It is too much. My arteries, although they are soft, beat too fast. I shall have to start taking notes on my old age.

APRIL

Marinette's face when someone has passed her a counterfeit coin is worth a good five francs.

Parc Monceau. Silence surrounded by noise.
    A pigeon will not tolerate a neighbor on his branch.
    The sun hides behind the trunk of a tree.
    The pigeons perched with their elbows resting on the edge of the sky.

Peasants. They never eat eggs. They do as long as they are children and go to school; but they are disgusted with them as soon as they are grown. Besides, eggs can be sold, they bring in money.

Maman still has a great deal of life in her, a sort of ligneous life. She will make another Honorine.

My faithfulness as a husband, a comical thing, adds to my literary reputation.

Barfleur

Mme. Alix, fishmonger, says to her son-in-law:
"Don't go putting your cap on the table where one eats!"
A little sheepish, he removes it, and, by way of excusing himself, tells me that Mme. Alix is a superior woman.
How difficult it is to explain what you work at!
"So, you write?"
"All the time."
"And, to do your work, you don't have to go to Paris?"
"No, I don't. On the contrary."
"You make a lot of money!"
How deny it without casting away all honor? "Well, as for you, you are a fishmonger, are you not?"
By the third give-and-take you are perspiring. In order to have done with it, you say that you have a very pleasant occupation, which leaves you free; and even that you make a lot of money. You add that you have been decorated by the Legion of Honor and that you belong to a certain Academy.
They have noticed the decoration, but, seeing no reason for it, they would as soon not talk about it. At last they make up their minds:
"Well! I see you have made your way in the world."
The Academy means nothing to them, even when they hear it brings in 3000 francs.
"Rostand also, of whom you have of course heard—"
They nod, but I can tell by their eyes that they are ignorant of his very existence. You experience a pleasant minute or so, in this country.

MAY

A beautiful style should not be seen.

One should write as one breathes. A flowing breath, with its slow and its precipitate rhythms, always natural—that is the symbol of a good style.

All we owe the reader is clarity. He must accept originality, irony, violence, even if he doesn't like them. He does not have the right to judge of these. One might say that they are not his concern.

The Luxembourg gardens are nothing but a dome of leaves under which people dream.

Galerie Durand-Ruel. *Les Nymphéas*, a series of waterscapes, by Claude Monet. I find nothing to say. Obviously, it is pretty; but I can't very well say: "It is pretty, especially in the oval frames." There is an abyss between this art and ours.

A shabbily-dressed young man sits gazing fixedly, through half-closed eyes. I wish I could see what he sees.

It is painting for women. They cannot deny it. It is too pretty: nature does not produce that.

A terrible desire to leave, in the manner of having gone on a trip in order to be able to say: "I was there."

I can no longer walk from one end of the Tuileries to the other. I am obliged to sit down and give two sous to the old women who sell lilies-of-the-valley.

Philippe writes that maman is no longer always right in her mind. And Antoine writes that he is about to start rehearsals of *La Bigote*.

Life continues. My pen has a thin, funereal sound.

Nothing is more disliked than originality. An audience of original minds would not stand for anything but a commonplace lecture.

Chaumot

Maman. Her illness, her stage-setting of the armchair. She gets into bed when she hears Marinette's footsteps.

Her moments of lucidity. That is when she does her best play-acting. She trembles, rubs her hands, clacks her teeth, and, with eyes slightly wild, says:

"All I am going to do! I'll get at it right away. I'm going to get to work. When a person works—" She does a darn in her stocking.

A handsome old woman still—the face of a witch with clear features, or of an old woman in a gypsy van, with her wavy white hair.

If you send her asparagus, she gives it to the rabbits.

The women come to visit her like thieves. She hasn't a chemise left, or a sheet: she has given everything away.

Finally, she says: "I don't need money any more."

Sometimes I am under the impression that she is thirty years younger, setting upon Poil de Carotte with her cunning. But she says, with false gentleness:

"You're scolding me? It's really pretty tough, what you're saying to me!"

She closes the door in Ragotte's face, but Ragotte says: "Monsieur sent me."

The door opens.

Three states: lucidity, enfeeblement, real suffering. In the lucid state, she is still entirely Mme. Lepic.

She sends Philippe to tell us: "Don't leave! I feel that I am going!"

In the manner in which she holds one's hands and presses them, there is almost an intent to hurt.

When winter comes, he says, I feel like getting married. It is cold, and the restaurant is a good way off. I feel the need of a home. When spring comes, it passes.

A walk to Chatou.

In the grass, a little woman sufficient unto herself. She has come from far on a bicycle, with a black poodle. She makes up a bouquet of yellow flowers. The poodle guards her. When she has finished, she goes away. Happiness found in activity and unconcern.

Yesterday, I saw bliss: after a day of burning heat, a cluster of rose bushes receiving a continuous jet from a sprinkling can. "Yes, yes! It feels good!" they were saying with all their leaves.

It is the "beautiful descriptions" that have given me a taste for descriptions in three words.

Fairly good critiques might be possible if the critic were not always concerned with having things sound either better or worse than he actually finds them to be.

JUNE

Charles-Louis Philippe gives the impression that he is cheating us, and that he is not all that soft about humankind.

If chastity is not a virtue, surely it is a force.

What is exact cannot help but be subtle.

Chaumot

Maman wants to go and see the leaves floating in the well, to sit on the well curb. In the cupboard, she keeps something that she looks at from time to time. Eyes wild, she gets up suddenly from her armchair and goes to the garden.

Her legs, swollen with varicose veins, are painful to look at. The head remains handsome, with wavy hair.

JULY

"Forgive me! Forgive me!" maman says to me.

She holds out her arms and draws me to her. She falls at the feet of Marinette, whom she has not appreciated; she throws herself at the feet of Amélie, of her two daughters.

To these "Forgive me! Forgive me!"'s, all I can find as a reply is, "I'll come back tomorrow."

Afterwards, she gives herself violent blows on the head with her fist.

AUGUST

On the 5th, death of maman, buried the 7th. Visit from Capus. He had an automobile accident at Lormes. He arrives all set up by his accident, in the midst of ours.

Last words heard from my mother:

"Are you coming back soon? Thanks for coming to see me."

Mme. Robin, Juliette, had just gone. Baïe, Marinette and I had left her on the garden bench. Amélie had followed us. I had just received the telegram from Capus announcing his visit. She, from her bench, kept turning around in my direction, trying to guess what this telegram could be about.

I do not believe that she threw herself into the well. She had gone to sit on the curb, after having said a few words to someone who was passing by. She knotted the chain; then, the seizure. She fell backward. A little fellow on a cart, near-by, saw her. Amélie's maid heard "Plunk!" She saw her in the well, she said, fallen on her back, and she screamed.

I come running on leaden legs. I pass others who are running. I cast aside any hat and my Rostand cane. And I bend over the edge of the well.

A skirt floating on the water, a slight eddying such as there is when one has drowned an animal. No human face.

I naturally want to go down in the bucket at the end of the chain. The chain is rolled up. My boots are absurdly long and turn up the way fish do at the bottom of a pail.

Cries of "Don't go down!" A voice: "There is no danger!"

At last, a ladder is brought. I can hardly free my feet of the bucket. The ladder does not reach the water. With one hand, I try to seize that dead thing that does not move. The head is under water. The dress tears. I come up again. All I did was wet my foot. What must I have looked like, coming out of the well?

Two men go down. They are able to seize her and carry her up.

A somewhat frightening face comes out of the well.

She is carried to her bed. Marinette is still here.

Not a tear. I do automatically what I would do if I were controlling myself.

Spent the night near the body as I did for papa. Why? The same impression.

Whether she died by accident or committed suicide, what is the difference from the religious standpoint? In the one case, it is she who did wrong, in the other case, it is God.

There is the consecrated grave. Who will win, the bigot or the freemasons?

There is a slipper that hasn't been found.

What is left? Work.

The slightest annoyance unhinges me. A material event, such as an accident, a death, does not move me. I should prefer to be moved.

"A sorrow, a terrible sorrow." Why, no! It doesn't take shape immediately like physical pain. There is pain that, after the event, takes a long time to penetrate, to settle in.

The thunder at the edge of a cloud impresses me.

We are not even responsible for our sorrows,

Is God's being incomprehensible the weightiest reason we can advance for His existence?

Our embarrassment in the face of sorrow is what marks us out most strongly as men of letters. The slightest thing is enough to bring it on: a telegram of condolence from a stranger.

She was being playful, bending over the edge of the well in order to see the wet grasses glistening down there, kneeling in order to worry Amélie, crying out and raising her arms in the air so that the maid came running; then saying she had done it to chase a hen out of the garden. The mother of an ironist should not make jokes. No, she was not play-acting, although I was the first to think that was exactly what it looked like.

Poil de Carotte: "Well, you asked for the truth. I am giving it to you."

"Yes, you give it to me. It is interesting."

Have read the letters that papa wrote to her. Tenderness. And he says: "I pray God that . . ." Falsehood is never eternal.

Death is not an artist.

Unfathomable accident.

The play of the moonlight on the sheet.

Not a scratch on her. She must have dropped like a dead weight.

It is a rather complicated way of making me an orphan.

Truth is always disenchanting. Art is here in order to falsify it.

When I was ten years old I didn't dream. Or, rather, I wanted to be happy day by day, no matter how. It is no secret that, for twenty years, I have had the best of wives. My other dreams have never come true. No doubt it would be better not to say it, but it is thanks to her that, now and then, it has seemed to me that my other dreams might also be coming true.

Life is neither long nor short: it has long-drawn-out moments.

OCTOBER

Truth exists only in the imagination. Choice in truth lies in observation. A poet is an observer who re-creates immediately. The proof of this is that, when next he looks at people, he does not recognize them.

Wonderful opening night [of *La Bigote*]. Three curtain calls after the first act, four after the second. Ovation. Have never seen my friends so moved.

NOVEMBER

Crisis. Shortness of breath; disgust with everything. Death might come in an hour or in ten years. To think that I should prefer ten years!

DECEMBER

Saw Rostand again, after nine years. I kiss him on the cheek. He kisses me in the manner of a priest, and I get an impression of something round, like a Holland cheese. He is unrecognizable. He looks like a nice, fat man. Subject to migraines. You feel that the headaches have become unnecessary. Short-sighted, he comes close and peers to see if you have aged.

Romanticism wanted to introduce lyricism into the theatre. Realism wanted to do the same thing, but with a concentrated lyricism, ringing true.

Realism has conquered only in details.

I reproach Shakespeare with not knowing French. So much the better! That makes two beautiful languages, and makes one want to learn them.

Ugliness predominates, because life is not beautiful. The public knows nothing about either beauty or charm. They like verse, yes, when it comes from the lips of a pretty actress or one of their favorite actors, (which amounts to the same thing), or when there is music around it.

Conventions: in this sense the theatre is bigger than life.

The public confuses verisimilitude with truth.

There must be realism in the highest kind of lyricism.

The romantic looks at a large mirror and believes it to be the sea. The realist looks at the sea and believes it to be a mirror. But the man with a straightforward mind says, in front of the mirror: "It is a mirror", and, in front of the sea: "It is the sea."

A loose style—*there* is charm.

If there is something more unpleasant than pushiness, it is a display of modesty.

As soon as one has looked it in the face, death is gentle to understand.

Ill, I should like to say profound, slightly historical things, which my friends would repeat; but it makes me nervous.

It is not for a sign from God that I ask. If only I saw men act as they speak, I should at once be moved.

"Monsieur must have been good-looking, when he was young," says the maid.

To lose the appetite for reading.

I wrote *La Bigote*, not as a polemic, but to please myself. It is written. Let it deliver what it can.

In me, I have a disease to observe. It is almost as good as a crime in the family.

The brain that is going, impossible to hold back. The dandelion might as well try to hold back its fluff.

Already, I am developing a taste for walking in cemeteries.

The mystery of death is enough. All those things one attaches to it are stage tricks.

Ah! that man passing by looks sick too! It is the opposite of my decoration. Then I used to say: "What! He also!"

1910

*I don't understand life at all, but I don't say it is impossible
that God may understand it a little.*

By the end of February, severe worsening of JR's condition. May 22: death of JR in
Paris of arteriosclerosis. Burial in Chitry.

JANUARY

My heart beats like a buried miner trying, by means of irregular
knocks, to signal that he is still alive.

The detestable pleasure, almost in the nature of a restorative, of
venting one's bad humor upon others.

Walk in the Bois.
  The old women buried in the depths of carriages.
  The fine swans, clothed in their snow.

My name is on all the walls, on the posters of the *Paris-Journal*, but
in the streetcar not a soul knows me.

Snow on water: silence upon silence.

What is the good of these notebooks? No one tells the truth, not even the one who writes it down.

FEBRUARY

Certain liars have such a need of lying that one takes pity on them and helps them along.

Absorbed as a cat watching on the ceiling the reflection of a lamp.

I cannot make up my mind to put an end to my difficulties by calling in God.

Marinette weeps for the two of us, and, as for me, I help her a little.

Is it because I was the last to enter the Académie Goncourt that I shall be the first to leave it? Peculiar sort of balance!

Yesterday, Fantec gave me an auscultation. We laughed like fools as his ears moved over my back. He had to begin again two or three times. Nothing in the lungs. The heart is too large. He could hear the valves galloping. That put an end to my laughter.

Between my brain and me there is always a layer that I cannot penetrate.

And then I wrote *La Bigote*. Mme. Lepic is waiting. But why did *he* let me write *La Bigote*?

Besides, I'm through. I could begin all over again and do it better, but no one would notice the difference.

Better make an end.

MARCH

I don't understand life at all, but I don't say it is impossible that God may understand it a little.

Death of Moréas. Is it my turn?

He was a poet who betrayed his country, wrote a few fine lines of verse, and called me a fool.

APRIL

Last night I wanted to get up. Dead weight. A leg hangs outside. Then a trickle runs down my leg. I allow it to reach my heel before I make up my mind. It will dry in the sheets, the way it did when I was Poil de Carotte.

INDEX OF PROPER NAMES